Irregular Warfare
Special Study

4 August 2006

PREFACE

This report provides study results, analysis, conclusions, and recommendations concerning doctrinal implications of Irregular Warfare.

This report provides study results, analysis, conclusions, and recommendations concerning doctrinal implications of Irregular Warfare (IW) as introduced/described in the *2006 Quadrennial Defense Review* (2006 QDR) report and the subsequent IW roadmap. Specifically this study identifies current joint doctrinal treatment of IW and its aspects, to include content of ongoing revision efforts; identifies any joint doctrinal voids concerning IW and proposes courses of action for resolving identified voids; and identifies terminology implications/doctrinal issues related to IW.

The Joint Staff requested this study, via a memorandum approved by the Director for Operational Plans and Joint Force Development (J-7), Subject: Request for Irregular Warfare Special Study, dated 5 June 2006.

Data was gathered and analyzed from both approved US policy as well as joint doctrine publications and additional sources.

Pertinent data was gathered from Federal documents, to include the *National Military Strategy*, *National Defense Strategy*, and *National Security Strategy*; from approved joint publications, emerging joint doctrine, Department of Defense directives, Chairman of the Joint chiefs of Staff instructions; North Atlantic Treaty Organization publications; Service doctrine and other sources.

Analysis of the data was conducted to identify doctrinal treatment of IW and its aspects, and identify any joint doctrinal voids.

Based on the data, conclusions and recommendations are made.

Conclusions were drawn regarding the doctrinal implications of IW. Finally, recommendations were made regarding the joint doctrinal treatment of IW and courses of action proposed for resolving identified joint doctrinal voids.

TABLE OF CONTENTS

EXECUTIVE SUMMARY

This report provides study results, research, analysis, conclusions, and recommendations concerning doctrinal implications of Irregular Warfare (IW) as introduced/described in the *2006 Quadrennial Defense Review* (2006 QDR) report and the subsequent *Quadrennial Defense Review Irregular Warfare (IW) Roadmap*. Specifically this study identifies current joint doctrinal treatment of IW and its aspects, to include content of ongoing revision efforts; identifies any joint doctrinal voids concerning IW and proposes courses of action for resolving identified voids; and identifies terminology implications/doctrinal issues related to IW.

The study used a systematic approach by gathering pertinent information and then analyzing it in relation to IW. Thorough research and data collection was conducted on IW. Analysis centered on IW terminology and possible doctrinal voids and redundancies within the 10 IW activities (aspects) listed in the IW roadmap and, as a minimum, their associated joint publications (JPs). Conclusions were drawn regarding the doctrinal implications of IW. Finally, recommendations were made regarding the joint doctrinal treatment of IW and courses of action proposed for resolving identified joint doctrinal voids.

Major findings are:

The National Security Strategy of the United States of America, published the same month as the 2006 QDR and the National Military Strategic Plan for the War on Terrorism published the month before the 2006 QDR make no mention of IW.

The working definitions of IW in the IW roadmap, current Joint Capability Area (JCA) Lexicon, draft JCA Lexicon, and draft NATO usage are not harmonized and in fact are contradictory.

Without an accepted and approved definition, IW cannot be included in joint doctrine. Historically, terms such as Military Operations Other Than War (MOOTW) that lack a precise definition that derives from broad consensus, are short-lived. Approved concepts such as "dominant maneuver" often fail to make the transition from concept to doctrine.

As the primary focus of UW is on political-military objectives, it is unclear how this differs from the working definition of IW which states "... [the] objective [is] the credibility and/or legitimacy of the relevant political authority...."

As a practical matter, the IW concept and descriptions available are too immature to develop a joint doctrine construct now and the potential for future development is doubtful based on the analysis presented in this study.

Major recommendations are:

Reject addressing IW as a term or construct in joint doctrine. Do not define it or include it in JP 1-02 *Department of Defense Dictionary of Military and Associated Terms* **or any other joint publications.**

USJFCOM assess the need for and develop and submit a **joint doctrine project proposal on Counterinsurgency**.

USJFCOM assess the need for and develop and submit a **joint doctrine project proposal on Counterterrorism (CT) and Combating Terrorism (CbT)**. Consider as an option to change the title and scope of JP 3-07.2 *Antiterrorism* to include CbT and CT.

Conduct an **early formal assessment of JP 3-05** *Doctrine for Joint Special Operations* prior to June 2008. Specifically assess the need for a discussion of operational level authoritative guidance for joint special operations support to conventional forces.

Conduct an **early formal assessment of JP 3-07.1** *Joint Tactics, Techniques, and Procedures for Foreign Internal Defense (FID)* prior to January 2008. Assess the need for a discussion of operational level authoritative guidance for general purpose forces to conduct Foreign Internal Defense and to train, equip, and advise large numbers of foreign security forces

USJFCOM develop and submit a **joint doctrine project proposal on stability operations** and military support to Stability, Security, Transition, and Reconstruction operations.

Determine through approved JP maintenance assessments if a void has in fact emerged regarding transnational criminal activities that support or sustain IW and the law enforcement activities to counter them.

Continue the normal maintenance on doctrine regarding Civil-Military Operations, Psychological Operations, Information Operations, and intelligence and Counterintelligence Operations.

CHAPTER I

INTRODUCTION

SECTION A. PURPOSE

This report provides study results, research, analysis, conclusions, and recommendations concerning doctrinal implications of Irregular Warfare (IW) as introduced/described in the *2006 Quadrennial Defense Review* (2006 QDR) report and the subsequent *Quadrennial Defense Review Irregular Warfare (IW) Roadmap* herein referred to as the IW roadmap. Specifically this study identifies current joint doctrinal treatment of IW and its aspects, to include content of ongoing revision efforts; identifies any joint doctrinal voids concerning IW and proposes courses of action for resolving identified voids; and identifies terminology implications/ doctrinal issues related to IW. A copy of the memorandum from the Director for Operational Plans and Joint Force Development (Joint Staff J-7) requesting this study is at Enclosure A.

SECTION B. METHODOLOGY

1. The study used a systematic approach by gathering pertinent information and then analyzing it in relation to IW as presented in the 2006 QDR and IW roadmap. The IW roadmap identified the following 10 activities (aspects) as an illustrative list. These 10 activities (aspects) were reviewed for doctrinal implications:

    a. Insurgency and counterinsurgency (COIN).

    b. Terrorism and counterterrorism (CT).

    c. Unconventional warfare (UW).

    d. Foreign internal defense (FID).

    e. Stability, security, transition, and reconstruction (SSTR) operations.

    f. Transnational criminal activities that support or sustain IW and the law enforcement activities to counter them.

    g. Civil-military operations (CMO).

    h. Psychological operations (PSYOP).

    i. Information operations (IO).

    j. Intelligence and counterintelligence operations.

2. The analysis described the doctrinal treatment of IW and its listed activities (aspects) and identified joint doctrinal voids. Conclusions were

then drawn and recommendations were made based on the information and analytical results.

SECTION C. STUDY OUTLINE

1. Research and Data Collection

a. The following publications, directives, instructions, and relevant materials were identified:

(1) The *National Military Strategy*, *National Defense Strategy*, *National Security Strategy*, and other Federal level documents were searched and reviewed.

(2) The Joint Electronic Library (JEL) and associated indices were searched to identify Department of Defense (DOD) directives and instructions, Chairman of the Joint Chiefs of Staff (CJCS) instructions (including the *Universal Joint Task List*), approved and emerging joint doctrine, and approved doctrine projects relevant to this study.

(3) Service, multi-Service, and North Atlantic Treaty Organization (NATO) doctrine were searched to identify information relevant to this study.

b. The Naval Postgraduate School Center on Terrorism and Irregular Warfare and the United States Military Academy Military Art and Science Major Irregular Warfare Specialty Track websites were reviewed for pertinent information. General internet searches as well as searches against the Defense Technical Information Center (DTIC) databases were conducted for additional information.

c. CJCS Joint Professional Military Education (JPME) Special Areas of Emphasis (SAE), Joint Concepts, and Joint Capability Areas (JCAs) were searched to identify information relevant to this study.

2. Analysis, Conclusions, and Recommendations

a. The analysis centered on IW terminology and the 10 IW activities (aspects) listed in the IW roadmap and, as a minimum, their associated joint publications (JPs).

b. Conclusions were drawn regarding the construct of IW and the adequacy of approved and emerging joint doctrine with respect to the 10 IW activities (aspects) listed in the IW roadmap.

c. Finally, recommendations were made regarding courses of action for resolving identified doctrinal voids and terminology implications/doctrinal issues.

d. A number of documents at the Federal, DOD, and CJCS levels that are in development or revision may have a major impact on this study.

(1) The IW roadmap directs that the "Commander of the United States Special Operations Command, in coordination with the Chairman of the Joint Chiefs of Staff, the Commanders of the other Combatant Commands, and the Chiefs of the Military Services, will provide to the Deputy Secretary of Defense by December 15, 2006 a joint concept for IW."

(2) Action offices identified in the IW roadmap will develop action/implementation plans and other documents to execute their specific responsibilities as outlined in the IW roadmap.

e. The analysis, conclusions, and recommendations are based on available information as of 1 July 2006. The dynamics of the research arena should be considered during approval and application of the recommendations.

SECTION D. ASSUMPTIONS

This study assumed the following:

1. IW, as defined in the IW roadmap, is an emerging concept with a nonauthoritative, "working" definition. Without an approved definition and concept, any analysis will be incomplete. An approved definition is required before any term can be accepted into joint doctrine.

2. Any IW construct will introduce some doctrinal/terminology implications. This includes a potential conflict with the current definition of unconventional warfare.

3. Not all activities of IW can or should be performed by US military forces. There would not be joint doctrine for those activities.

SECTION E. ADMINISTRATIVE

Questions concerning this study may be addressed to the United States Joint Forces Command Joint Warfighting Center using the address below or by telephone at DSN 668-6062/6955, Commercial (757) 203-6062/6955, or FAX 668-6198.

US postal mailing address:

Commander
USJFCOM Joint Warfighting Center
ATTN: JT10 (Doctrine Group)
116 Lake View Parkway
Suffolk, Virginia 23435-2697

CHAPTER II

RESEARCH AND DATA SUMMARIES

> *"Since the attacks of September 11, 2001, our Nation has fought a global war against violent extremists who use terrorism as their weapon of choice, and who seek to destroy our free way of life. Our enemies seek weapons of mass destruction and, if they are successful, will likely attempt to use them in their conflict with free people everywhere. Currently, the struggle is centered in Iraq and Afghanistan, but we will need to be prepared and arranged to successfully defend our Nation and its interests around the globe for years to come. This 2006 Quadrennial Defense Review is submitted in the fifth year of this long war."*

SECTION A. RESEARCH ON IRREGULAR WARFARE

This section provides research and data collection conducted on IW. This involved identifying and reviewing Federal, DOD, CJCS, Service, multi-Service, and NATO publications, directives, instructions, documents, and relevant materials. Internet searches were conducted against military, government, and general websites and databases for additional information. Finally, CJCS JPME SAE, Joint Concepts, and JCAs were searched to identify information relevant to this study.

1. **Federal Documents.** National level documents were reviewed to obtain information regarding IW.

   a. IW is not mentioned in *The National Security Strategy of the United States of America*, March 2006.

   b. IW is not mentioned in *The National Military Strategic Plan for the War on Terrorism*, February 2006. Irregular challenges are mentioned.

   c. IW is not mentioned in *The National Strategy for Victory in Iraq*, November 2005.

   d. IW is not mentioned in *The National Strategy for Combating Terrorism*, February 2003.

   e. IW is not mentioned in The *National Defense Strategy of The United States of America*, March 2005, but it does mention irregular challenges in the context of an array of traditional, irregular, catastrophic, and disruptive capabilities and methods that threaten US interests.

f. IW is not mentioned in *The National Military Strategy of the United States of America*, 2004, but it does mention irregular challenges.

g. IW is not mentioned in any DOD directive or instruction.

h. IW is not mentioned in any Chairman of the Joint Chiefs of Staff instruction or manual. (This includes the *Universal Joint Task List*.)

i. IW is mentioned in the Quadrennial Defense Review Report 2006, 24 times. A working definition of IW approved by Deputy Secretary of Defense on 17 April 2006 is provided in the IW roadmap.

> *"Irregular warfare is a form of warfare that has as its objective the credibility and/or legitimacy of the relevant political authority with the goal of undermining or supporting that authority. Irregular warfare favors indirect approaches, though it may employ the full range of military and other capabilities to seek asymmetric approaches, in order to erode an adversary's power, influence, and will."*

2. **Joint Doctrine.** IW is not defined nor mentioned in current joint doctrine, revisions of joint doctrine, joint doctrine under development, or approved joint doctrine projects.

3. **Service Doctrine.** IW is not defined nor mentioned in current Service doctrine. The June 2006 (Final Draft) FM 3-24/FMFM 3-24 *Counterinsurgency* mentions IW twice. It appears to be used interchangeably with COIN and guerrilla warfare and is not further defined or used in a consistent context.

4. **North Atlantic Treaty Organization Doctrine**

a. IW is mentioned in three NATO publications - *NATO Handbook For Coalition Operations*, February 2004; *NATO Handbook For Coalition Operations (Land)* June 2004; and AJP-3.2, *Allied Land Operations*, 2d Study Draft, February 2006.

b. The first two publications only mention IW. The Draft of AJP-3.2 places IW as a subset of "stability operations." It does not define IW, but provides the following discussion:

> *"Irregular <u>warfare</u> denotes a form of conflict where one or more protagonists adopts irregular methods. Irregular <u>troops</u> are any combatants not formally enlisted in the armed forces*

*of a nation-state or other legally-constituted entity. Stability
operations in this category include actions to counter irregular
troops or forces employing irregular methods, counter
terrorism, and assistance to friendly irregular forces. It is
likely that in countering an irregular adversary the peace
support activities mentioned will be conducted, but specific
offensive and defensive operations will be utilized to counter
that adversary and that the principles of COIN might be
used."*

5. **Internet Research**

a. The Naval Postgraduate School Center on Terrorism and Irregular
Warfare and the United States Military Academy Military Art and Science
Major Irregular Warfare Specialty Track websites also were reviewed for
pertinent information. Nothing was found regarding the definition,
scope, elements, or activities regarding IW as described in the IW
roadmap.

b. General internet searches as well as searches against the DTIC
databases were conducted for additional information. Research revealed
that IW is used loosely as a synonym for unconventional warfare,
asymmetric warfare, guerrilla warfare, partisan warfare, nontraditional
warfare, low intensity conflict, insurgency, rebellion, revolt, civil war,
insurrection, revolutionary warfare, internal war, counter insurgency,
subversive war, war within a population, intrastate war, internal
development, internal security, internal defense, stability, law and order,
nation building, state building, small war, peacemaking, peacekeeping,
fourth generation warfare (4GW), and global war on terror (GWOT). Little
consistency, clarity, or consensus was found regarding a definition of IW,
usage of IW, or of IW as a construct.

c. The controversy over IW terminology is nothing new. After 44
years of discussion, a definitive definition still has not emerged.

*"To sever orthodox and irregular warfare is artificial and at
best a convenience used to classify relative conditions of a
specific time. Conflict is actually a spectrum which extend
from diplomatic action (no use of force) to orthodox warfare
(use of conventional military units in "War"). Between these
two extremes lies irregular warfare. There is no standard
terminology for the subject of this study. The whole subject
has been called unconventional warfare (James D. Atkinson),
fourth dimensional warfare (Frank R. Barnett), irregular
warfare, cold war, and situations short of war. Each term has
its own peculiars meaning to each author." (Holliday, Sam C.*

and Dabezies, Pierre C., *Irregular Warfare* in a Nutshell, Fort Leavenworth, Kansas, 1962)

6. **Joint Professional Military Education.** The Chairman approves a list of CJCS JPME SAEs annually. SAEs highlight the concerns of the Office of the Secretary of Defense (OSD), the Services, combatant commands, Defense agencies, and the Joint Staff regarding coverage of specific joint subject matter in the Professional Military Education colleges. They help maintain the currency and relevance of the colleges' JPME curricula and provide an independent view of what those curricula should address. Colleges and schools evaluate each approved SAE and, where they deem feasible and appropriate, incorporate them in their curricula; however, inclusion is not required.

a. The list of approved 2006 CJCS JPME SAEs include Counter Ideological Support for Terrorism (CIST). The SAE describes the CIST concept as integral to the US government and military strategy for the War on Terrorism (WOT). CIST attacks extremist ideology, the enemy's strategic center of gravity. All military members should have an understanding of the principle framework of the WOT strategy, including CIST. JPME curricula should challenge students to investigate the five elements of the DOD role in CIST (security, IO, humanitarian support, military-to-military contacts, and conduct of operations) and provide students with an awareness of the culture, customs, language, and philosophy of the enemy.

b. Research revealed no documentation of and little information about CIST.

c. IW is nominated by the Joint Staff J-3 as a 2007 CJCS JPME SAE.

7. **Joint Concepts**

a. IW is not mentioned in *The Capstone Concept for Joint Operations*, August 2005, but it does mention irregular methods in that complex and adaptive adversaries will likely employ traditional, irregular, disruptive, and catastrophic methods singularly or in combinations, which are intended to keep the future joint force from being successful across the range of military operations.

b. A Joint Operating Concept (JOC) for IW is under development and scheduled for completion 15 December 2006. The US Marine Corps Combat Development Command and US Special Operations Command Center for Knowledge and Futures *Multi-Service Concept for Irregular Warfare,* Draft Version 1.7.4, 9 June 2006, serves as a baseline for the IW JOC.

8. Joint Capability Areas

a. The *Refined Joint Capability Areas Tier 1 and Supporting Tier 2 Lexicon*, 24 August 2005 defines "Joint Special Operations & Irregular Warfare" as:

> *"The ability to conduct operations in hostile, denied, or politically sensitive environments to achieve military, diplomatic, informational, and/or economic objectives employing military capabilities for which there is no broad conventional force requirement. These operations may require low visibility, clandestine, or covert capabilities that are applicable across the range of military operations. They can be conducted independently of or in conjunction with operations of conventional forces or other government agencies, and may include operations through, with, or by indigenous or surrogate forces."*

It further defines Joint Irregular Operations/Warfare as:

> *"Joint Irregular Operations/Warfare involve conventional and special operations forces conducting operations to counter the activities of irregular forces. Joint Irregular Operations/ Warfare include elements of, but are not limited to, foreign internal defense and counterinsurgency, counterterrorism, unconventional warfare, information operations and stability operations undertaken to defeat adversaries who conduct activities and employ methods not sanctioned by international law or customs of war. Joint Irregular Operations/Warfare involve all elements of national power (diplomatic, informational, military, and economic) and as such are joint, combined, multinational, and interagency in its scope. Joint Irregular Operations/Warfare is generally protracted and requires sustained political-military willpower to effectively conduct."*

The *JCA Tier 1 & Tier 2 Taxonomy*, 24 August 2005 places "Joint Irregular Warfare" as a Tier 2 JCA under "Joint Special Operations & Irregular Operations."

b. The *Proposed Joint Capability Areas Tier 1 and Supporting Tier 2 Lexicon* (Mar 06 refinement effort results), defines "Joint Special Operations & Irregular Warfare" as:

"The ability to conduct operations that apply or counter means other than direct, traditional forms of combat involving peer-to-peer fighting between the regular armed forces of two or more countries. The ability to conduct operations in hostile, denied, or politically sensitive environments to achieve military, diplomatic, informational, and/or economic objectives employing military capabilities for which there is no broad conventional force requirement. These operations may require low visibility, clandestine, or covert capabilities that are applicable across the range of military operations. They can be conducted independently of or in conjunction with operations of conventional forces or other government agencies, and may include operations through, with, or by indigenous or surrogate forces."

It further defines IW as:

"The ability to conduct warfare that has as its objective the credibility and/or legitimacy of the relevant political authority with the goal of undermining or supporting that authority. Irregular warfare favors indirect approaches, though it may apply the full range of military and other capabilities to seek asymmetric approaches, in order to erode an adversary's power, influence and will."

The Draft *JCA Tier 1 & Tier 2 Taxonomy*, April 2006 places "Irregular Warfare" as a Tier 2 JCA under "Joint Special Operations & Irregular Warfare."

c. CJCS JCA Progress Report briefing dated 15 May 2006 to the Operations Deputies outlines this unresolved issue: "Irregular Ops / Irregular Warfare as a Tier 1 / 2 JCA vice an overarching concept that involves DoD resources across multiple Tier 1 JCAs." Four competing alternatives are presented to resolve this issue. Alternative two "Eliminates IW as a Tier 2 and moves FID to Joint Shaping and Counterinsurgency to Joint Stability Ops." The briefing recommended to "defer further adjudication of unresolved issues pending the development of a Department-wide JCA Implementation Plan." The briefing also states "Continue to review JCA evolution and **transition to joint doctrine when appropriate**."

9. **Legal Aspects**

a. The resources of the Army's Judge Advocate General's Center were searched for references to IW. Nothing was found regarding the definition, scope, elements, or activities regarding IW as described in the IW roadmap.

   b. Informal inquires also were made to the Army's Judge Advocate General's Center. They are not working on anything specific to IW. They focus on the law of warfare as it applies across the range of military operations.

SECTION B. RESEARCH ON ACTIVITIES (ASPECTS) OF IRREGULAR WARFARE

   This section summarizes information in joint doctrine regarding each of the 10 IW activities listed in the IW roadmap. Detailed information on each activity is found in Enclosures B through K.

1. **Insurgency and Counterinsurgency.** Insurgency and COIN are established terms in joint doctrine. While these terms appear in over 30 joint publications, there is almost no specific discussion in joint doctrine regarding them. Many joint publications that mention COIN refer back to FID, and while COIN is most frequently mentioned in FID, there is little discussion of specifics. The following definitions of COIN and insurgency appear in joint doctrine:

> **"counterinsurgency.** *Those military, paramilitary, political, economic, psychological, and civic actions taken by a government to defeat insurgency. (JP 1-02)"*

> **"insurgency.** *An organized movement aimed at the overthrow of a constituted government through use of subversion and armed conflict. (JP 1-02)"*

2. **Terrorism and Counterterrorism.** Terrorism and CT are established terms in joint doctrine. CT is mentioned in over 35 joint publications. CT is one of four actions of combating terrorism (CbT) — antiterrorism (AT) (defensive measures used to reduce the vulnerability to terrorist acts), CT (offensive measures taken to prevent, deter, preempt, and respond to terrorism), consequence management (CM) (preparation for and response to consequences of a terrorist incident), and intelligence support (collection or dissemination of terrorism-related information). These four actions are taken to oppose terrorism throughout the entire threat spectrum. CT is one of nine core tasks special operations forces (SOF) are specifically organized, trained, and equipped to accomplish. DOD plays an important role in domestic CT support to the Federal Bureau of Investigation (FBI). Although frequently mentioned in joint

doctrine, there is sparse discussion of CT in unclassified joint publications. The following definitions appear in joint doctrine:

> **"terrorism.** *The calculated use of unlawful violence or threat of unlawful violence to inculcate fear; intended to coerce or to intimidate governments or societies in the pursuit of goals that are generally political, religious, or ideological. (JP 1-02)"*

> **"counterterrorism.** *Operations that include the offensive measures taken to prevent, deter, preempt, and respond to terrorism. (JP 1-02)"*

3. **Unconventional Warfare**. UW is a well established program, defined as:

> *"A broad spectrum of military and paramilitary operations, normally of long duration, predominantly conducted through, with, or by indigenous or surrogate forces who are organized, trained, equipped, supported and directed in varying degrees by an external source. It includes, but is not limited to, guerrilla warfare, subversion, sabotage, intelligence activities, and unconventional assisted recovery. (JP 1-02)"*

A search of joint doctrine publications and resources for UW returned over 220 references in over 25 JPs. UW is primarily discussed in JP 3-05, *Doctrine for Joint Special Operations*. UW is unique in that it is special operations (SO) that can either be conducted as part of a geographic combatant commander's overall theater campaign, or as an independent, subordinate campaign. When conducted independently, the primary focus of UW is on political-military objectives and psychological objectives. UW includes military and paramilitary aspects of resistance movements. UW military activity represents the culmination of a successful effort to organize and mobilize the civil populace against a hostile government or occupying power. From the US perspective, the intent is to develop and sustain these supported resistance organizations and to synchronize their activities to further US national security objectives. SOF units do not create resistance movements. They advise, train, and assist indigenous resistance movements already in existence to conduct UW and when required, accompany them into combat. When UW operations support conventional military operations, the focus shifts to primarily military objectives; however the political and psychological implications remain. Operational and strategic staffs and commanders must guard against limiting UW to a specific set of circumstances or activities defined by either recent events or personal experience. **The most prevalent**

mistake is the belief that UW is limited to guerrilla warfare or insurgency.

4. **Foreign Internal Defense.** FID is a well established program, defined in JP 3-07.1, *Joint Tactics, Techniques, and Procedures for Foreign Internal Defense (FID)* as "the participation by civilian and military agencies of a government in any of the action programs taken by another government or other designated organization, to free and protect its society from subversion, lawlessness, and insurgency." A search of joint doctrine publications and resources for FID returned over 700 references in over 30 JPs.

5. **Stability, Security, Transition, and Reconstruction (SSTR) Operations.** SSTR operations is a relatively new term in DOD, not yet mentioned in joint doctrine.

    a. **IW Roadmap**. The IW roadmap describes SSTR operations as "operations conducted to set conditions for the establishment or restoration of order and to enable the transition of governmental and security functions to legitimate, and preferably indigenous, civil authorities. In SSTR operations, the principal role of U.S. military forces is to set security conditions."

    b. **DOD Policy**. Military support to SSTR is defined in DODD 3000.05, *Military Support for Stability, Security, Transition, and Reconstruction (SSTR) Operations*, as "Department of Defense activities that support U.S. Government plans for stabilization, security, reconstruction and transition operations, which lead to sustainable peace while advancing U.S. interests." DODD 3000.05 establishes "stability operations" as a "core US military mission" that provides DOD support to SSTR. It recognizes that stability operations provide a local population with security, restoration of essential services, and humanitarian assistance. DODD 3000.05 discusses the conduct of stability operations within the context of interagency coordination and coordination with intergovernmental and nongovernmental organizations. Further, it directs that plans for stability operations shall be included in all phases of joint operation plans.

    c. **Joint Doctrine**. DODD 3000.05 also directs the CJCS to establish joint doctrine for stability operations, which is being initiated through the revision of JP 3-0, *Joint Operations*. Per JP 3-0 Revision Approval Draft (RAD), stability operations are "missions, tasks, and activities which seek to maintain or reestablish a safe and secure environment and provide essential governmental services, emergency infrastructure reconstruction, or humanitarian relief." JP 3-0 RAD also establishes the application of stability operations throughout the notional phases of a major operation or campaign and describes its relationship between offensive and defensive operations. Further, stability operations do not encompass "types of joint operations" such as peace operations or foreign humanitarian assistance — stability operations may be part of those operations. Consequently, the "stability operations" construct in the JP 3-0 RAD is not a substitute for the term "military operations other than war (MOOTW)" that is being purged from joint doctrine through the consolidation of JP 3-07, *Joint Doctrine for Military Operations Other Than War*, with JP 3-0.

d. **Joint Concept**. The *Stability Operations Joint Operating Concept* was published on 9 September 2004. It does not define the term "stability operations," but states that stability operations will be conducted as part of a multinational and integrated, multiagency operation to provide security, initial humanitarian assistance, limited governance, restoration of essential public services, and other reconstruction assistance. It indicates that stability operations will be conducted during all phases of major operations involving combat. The *Military Support to Stabilization, Security, Transition, and Reconstruction Operations Joint Operating Concept* version 1.9 as of 22 June 2006 is currently being revised and staffed by US Joint Forces Command (USJFCOM) J9 and will replace the 2004 *Stability Operations Joint Operating Concept*.

e. **Army Doctrine**. The US Army conducts full-spectrum operations that are characterized as offensive, defensive, stability, and support operations. Stability operations are defined as those that "promote and protect US national interests by influencing the threat, political, and information dimensions of the operational environment through a combination of peacetime developmental, cooperative activities and coercive actions in response to crisis." (FM 3-07). They may take place before, during, and after offensive, defensive, and support operations. Specifically, stability operations are characterized as smaller-scale contingencies and peacetime military engagements (e.g., peace operations, FID, noncombatant evacuation operations). See Figure II-1 below. Field Manual 3-07, *Stability Operations and Support Operations*, February 2003, provides several considerations for planning and conducting stability operations.

TYPES OF MILITARY OPERATIONS	OFFENSE	DEFENSE	STABILITY	SUPPORT
TYPES OF STABILITY OPERATIONS AND THEIR SUBORDINATE FORMS	**Peace Operations** • Peacekeeping • Peace Enforcement • Operations in Support of Diplomatic Efforts **Foreign Internal Defense** • Indirect Support • Direct Support • Combat Operations **Security Assistance** **Humanitarian and Civic Assistance** **Support to Insurgencies** • Unconventional Warfare • Conventional Combat Actions **Support to Counterdrug Operations** • Detection and Monitoring • Host-Nation Support • C4 • Intelligence, Planning, CSS, Training, and Manpower Support • Reconnaissance		**Combatting Terrorism** • Antiterrorism • Counterterrorism **Noncombatant Evacuation Operations** **Arms Control** • Inspection • Protection • Destruction **Show of Force** • Increased Force Visibility • Exercises and Demonstrations	

Figure II-1. Types of Stability Operations (Army)

f. **JPME.** Military Support to SSTR operations is an approved 2006 CJCS JPME SAE. JPME curricula should challenge students to investigate the challenges and potential of focusing more intellectual effort on stability operations and the environments, especially regarding failed states in which they will be conducted. Stability operations must be examined thoroughly in the context of all elements of US national power and the interagency working group process.

6. **Transnational criminal activities that support or sustain IW and the law enforcement activities to counter them** are not defined nor explicitly discussed in joint doctrine.

7. **Civil-Military Operations.** CMO are discussed throughout current joint publications and associated documents. A search of joint doctrine publications and resources for CMO resulted in locating over 850 references in over 20 joint publications. JP 3-57, *Joint Doctrine for Civil-Military Operations*, defines CMO as:

> *"The activities of a commander that establish, maintain, influence, or exploit relations between forces, governmental and nongovernmental civilian organizations and authorities, and the civilian populace in a friendly, neutral, or hostile operational area in order to facilitate military operations, to consolidate and achieve operational US objectives. Civil-military operations may include performance by military*

forces of activities and functions normally the responsibility of the local, regional, or national government. These activities may occur prior to, during, or subsequent to other military actions. They may also occur, if directed, in the absence of other military operations. Civil-military operations may be performed by designated civil affairs, by other military forces, or by a combination of civil affairs and other forces."

CMO are not exclusive to the IW construct and are planned for and used in virtually all types of US military campaigns and operations.

8. **Psychological Operations.** PSYOP are addressed throughout joint publications and associated documents. A search of the joint electronic library resulted in locating over 300 references to PSYOP in 41 joint publications. JP 3-53, *Doctrine for Joint Psychological Operations*, addresses military PSYOP planning and execution in support of joint, multinational, and interagency efforts across the range of military operations. JP 3-53 defines PSYOP as:

> *"Planned operations to convey selected information and indicators to foreign audiences to influence their emotions, motives, objective reasoning, and ultimately the behavior of foreign governments, organizations, groups, and individuals. The purpose of psychological operations is to induce or reinforce foreign attitudes and behavior favorable to the originator's objectives."*

PSYOP are a vital part of the broad range of US diplomatic, informational, military, and economic activities. PSYOP characteristically are delivered as information for effect, used during peacetime and conflict, to inform and influence. PSYOP are a subset of IO.

9. **Information Operations.** IO are addressed throughout the joint doctrine hierarchy and other associated documents. A search of joint doctrine publications and resources resulted in locating 615 references to IO in 37 joint publications. JP 3-13, *Information Operations*, provides doctrine for IO planning, preparation, execution, and assessment in support of joint operations. JP 3-13 defines IO as:

> *"The integrated employment of the core capabilities of electronic warfare, computer network operations, psychological operations, military deception, and operations security, in concert with specified supporting and related capabilities, to influence, disrupt, corrupt or usurp adversarial*

human and automated decision making while protecting our own."

IO is not exclusive to the IW construct and is planned for and used in virtually all types of US military campaigns and operations. IO capabilities can produce effects and achieve objectives at all levels of war and across the range of military operations. The nature of the modern information environment complicates the identification of the boundaries between these levels. Therefore, at all levels, information activities, including IO, must be consistent with broader national security policy and strategic objectives.

10. **Intelligence and Counterintelligence Operations.** Intelligence and counterintelligence (CI) operations are broadly understood and discussed throughout the current joint doctrine hierarchy and in other associated documents. JP 2-0, *Joint Intelligence* is a capstone publication with an associated hierarchy. Nearly every joint publication discusses intelligence as it relates to the subject of that publication.

SECTION C. RELATED TERMS AND DEFINITIONS

This section provides specific terms that relate to the IW construct and its illustrated activities. They are listed to illustrate consistency or inconsistency of the definitions throughout DOD directives, CJCS instructions, and joint doctrine. Various definitions of IW uncovered during research are listed in Enclosure L.

1. **Conflict.** An armed struggle or clash between organized groups within a nation or between nations in order to achieve limited political or military objectives. Although regular forces are often involved, irregular forces frequently predominate. Conflict often is protracted, confined to a restricted geographic area, and constrained in weaponry and level of violence. Within this state, military power in response to threats may be exercised in an indirect manner while supportive of other instruments of national power. Limited objectives may be achieved by the short, focused, and direct application of force. (JP 1-02)

2. **Military Options.** A range of military force responses that can be projected to accomplish assigned tasks. Options include one or a combination of the following: civic action, humanitarian assistance, civil affairs, and other military activities to develop positive relationships with other countries; confidence building and other measures to reduce military tensions; military presence; activities to convey threats to adversaries as well as truth projections; military deceptions and psychological operations; quarantines, blockades, and harassment

operations; raids; intervention operations; armed conflict involving air, land, maritime, and strategic warfare operations; support for law enforcement authorities to counter international criminal activities (terrorism, narcotics trafficking, slavery, and piracy); support for law enforcement authorities to suppress domestic rebellion; and support for insurgency, counterinsurgency, and civil war in foreign countries. (JP 1-02)

3. **Stability Operations**. There are two published definitions of stability operations.

   a. Military and civilian activities conducted across the spectrum from peace to conflict to establish or maintain order in States and regions. (DODD 3000.05)

   b. An overarching term encompassing various military missions, tasks, and activities conducted outside the United States in coordination with other instruments of national power to maintain or reestablish a safe and secure environment, provide essential governmental services, emergency infrastructure reconstruction, and humanitarian relief. (Upon approval of the JP 3-0 revision, this term and definition will be included in JP 1-02.)

4. **Military support to Stability, Security, Transition and Reconstruction**. Department of Defense activities that support U.S. Government plans for stabilization, security, reconstruction and transition operations, which lead to sustainable peace while advancing U.S. interests. (DODD 3000.05)

CHAPTER III

ANALYSIS RESULTS

> *"The military strategic approach is to focus military operations in such a way as to assist other elements of national power to undermine the enemy center of gravity – violent extremist ideology. The Armed Forces of the United States will pursue direct and indirect methods to support activities to counter the enemy's ideology, support moderate alternatives, build capacities of partners, and attack the enemy to deny its key components."*
>
> National Military Strategic Plan for the War on Terrorism
> 1 February 2006

SECTION A. OVERVIEW

1. The analysis centered on IW terminology and possible doctrinal voids and redundancies within the 10 IW activities (aspects) listed in the IW roadmap and, as a minimum, their associated JPs.

    a. Current joint doctrinal treatment of IW and its activities (aspects), to include content of ongoing revision efforts are analyzed.

    b. Joint doctrinal voids concerning IW are identified as they apply to the 10 IW activities listed in the IW roadmap.

    c. Terminology implications/doctrinal issues related to IW are discussed.

2. Specifics of IW and its activities (aspects) and associated JPs will be addressed below.

SECTION B. THE IRREGULAR WARFARE CONSTRUCT

1. **Irregular Warfare Strategy and Policy.** The 2006 QDR, 17 April 2006, is the only document that mentions IW at the national strategy or policy level. **Most notably, *The National Security Strategy of the United States of America*, published the same month as the 2006 QDR and the *National Military Strategic Plan for the War on Terrorism* published the month before the 2006 QDR make no mention of IW.** DOD and CJCS policy also are silent on the subject.

2. Irregular Warfare Doctrine

a. IW is not mentioned in joint doctrine nor current Service doctrine. References in draft Service doctrine do not relate to the context of the IW working definition.

b. Doctrine describes activities that have a definable purpose. **There is no doctrinal value to arbitrarily grouping activities that are loosely related.** Unless there are underlying principles common to all activities, grouping them serves no purpose. Doctrine is inherently about principles. While we have immutable principles of war, and enduring fundamental elements operational design, which apply to the entire range of military operations, **it is difficult to imagine a new set of principles or elements that are unique to any construct of IW.** This analysis has not shown any value added by creating an IW construct.

c. **The working definitions of IW in the IW roadmap, current JCA Lexicon, draft JCA Lexicon, and draft NATO usage are not harmonized and in fact are contradictory.** Both the draft JCA Lexicon and NATO draft AJP-3.2 subordinate IW under "Joint Special Operations & Irregular Warfare" and "Stability Operations" categories respectively, while the IW roadmap proposes IW as an overarching concept.

d. The 10 activities (aspects) of IW as listed in the roadmap are neither inclusive, exclusive, nor exhaustive. These activities are conducted outside of the IW construct throughout the range of military operations. For example, military support to SSTR (i.e., stability operations), CT, and IO are executed now independent of IW. The 10 activities (aspects) that comprise IW appear to be cobbled together. Six of the 10 activities are SOF core tasks. PSYOP are one of five core capabilities of IO. It is not evident why PSYOP was singled out given it is a subset of IO. CT is only one of four actions of CbT. Again, it is unclear why the other three activities (aspects) are excluded. IO and intelligence are common to all operations. **The construct is far from a logical or neat "package."**

3. Irregular Warfare Terminology

a. The definition of IW is elusive. The long history of a lack of any consensus as to its meaning, and the loose usage as a synonym for many related terms, does not inspire confidence that an authoritative definition will emerge in the near future. **Without an accepted and approved definition, IW cannot be included in joint doctrine.** Historically, terms such as Military Operations Other Than War (MOOTW) that lack a precise definition that derives from broad consensus, are short-lived. Approved concepts such as "dominant maneuver" often fail to make the transition from concept to doctrine.

b. The term "irregular" implies there is an opposite type of warfare called "regular" warfare. The distinction between irregular and unconventional, and regular and conventional from the IW construct is unclear and would be difficult to articulate without ambiguity.

c. The construct of conventional and UW is well established in joint doctrine. **As the primary focus of UW is on political-military objectives, it is unclear how this differs from the working definition of IW which states "... [the] objective [is] the credibility and/or legitimacy of the relevant political authority...."**

d. The 2006 QDR states that "although U.S. military forces maintain their predominance in traditional warfare, they must also be improved to address irregular warfare; catastrophic terrorism employing weapons of mass destruction (WMD); and disruptive threats to the United States." When irregular warfare is considered within this construct of traditional, irregular, catastrophic, and disruptive challenges, this implies there also exists traditional warfare, catastrophic warfare, and disruptive warfare. This is not the case. It does not follow that irregular challenges in the context of an array of traditional, irregular, catastrophic, and disruptive challenges, creates four, or even two, types of warfare.

e. To succeed in the long war against terrorist networks, the United States often must take an indirect approach.

(1) Since Sun Tsu, the indirect approach has been part of the lexicon of warfare. The working definition of IW states that "IW favors indirect approaches." Basing a type of warfare primarily on only 1 of 17 elements of operational design (e.g., direct versus indirect) lacks rigor.

(2) As the quote at the beginning of this chapter implies, **focusing military operations to undermine the enemy center of gravity by indirect means is the strategic approach for the war on terrorism, not a new type of warfare**.

SECTION C. ACTIVITIES (ASPECTS) OF IRREGULAR WARFARE

The purpose for this section is to analyze information in joint doctrine regarding each of the 10 IW activities (aspects) illustrated in the IW roadmap.

1. **Insurgency and Counterinsurgency.** Insurgency and COIN are established terms in joint doctrine, yet there is **little specific discussion of these topics in joint doctrine**. The 2006 QDR calls for US general purpose forces (GPF) to conduct long-duration COIN operations. US Central Command (USCENTCOM) is currently conducting COIN operations in Iraq.

2. **Terrorism and Counterterrorism.** Terrorism and CT are established terms in joint doctrine. While the definitions are established, there is **little specific discussion of CT in joint doctrine**. CT is one of four actions of CbT and one of nine core SOF tasks. The 2006 QDR calls for US GPF to conduct long-duration CT operations.

    a. **Three of the four actions of CbT are thoroughly addressed in joint doctrine.** AT is covered in JP 3-07.2 *Antiterrorism*; CM is covered in JP 3-41 (Final Coordination Draft), *Chemical, Biological, Radiological, Nuclear, and High-Yield Explosives Consequence Management*; and intelligence support is covered in the JP 2 series.

    b. CT is a "Chairman's Commended Training Issue."

    c. DOD CT support to the FBI is not discussed in joint doctrine. Currently SOF perform this mission and it is unclear from the IW roadmap if this would be expanded to GPF.

3. **Unconventional Warfare.** UW is an established term in joint doctrine. The specific discussion of UW in joint doctrine is a subparagraph of just over one page in JP 3-05. UW is one of nine core SOF tasks. JP 3-05 was revised in December 2003. A preliminary assessment was completed in August 2005 recommending no early revision. **One notable suggestion was to expand the discussion of joint special operations support to conventional forces.** A formal assessment is scheduled for June 2008. The 2006 QDR does not call for US GPF to conduct UW.

4. **Foreign Internal Defense.** FID is well established and documented in joint doctrine. JP 3-07.1 is the dedicated publication on that subject and was revised in April 2004. A preliminary assessment of this publication was conducted in October 2005. The assessment did not recommend conducting an early formal assessment of JP 3-07.1. It recommended conducting a formal assessment of this publication in January 2008 unless significant relevant lessons learned surface or other compelling evidence warrants an urgent change.

    a. **The focus of JP 3-01.7 is on SOF conducting FID**. SOF are an integral part of FID and US Special Operations Command (USSOCOM) is the only combatant command with a legislatively-mandated FID core task. US GPF may contain and employ organic capabilities to conduct limited FID. Conventional forces can also participate in FID operations by providing specific expertise and various levels of support.

b. The IW roadmap calls for **US GPF to train, equip, and advise large numbers of foreign security forces**. The Multi-National Security Transition Command – Iraq, using GPF, is currently training, equipping, and advising large numbers of Iraqi security forces.

5. **Stability, Security, Transition, and Reconstruction Operations**. DODD 3000.05 establishes stability operations as the "core military mission" that supports US SSTR operations, i.e., SSTR operations are a US Government effort and stability operations comprise the military portion of that effort. JP 3-0 RAD, establishes basic joint doctrine on stability operations to satisfy the requirements of DODD 3000.05 — joint doctrine is in compliance with the policy.

a. The *Stability Operations Joint Operating Concept* is consistent with current policy on military support to SSTR operations and recently developed joint doctrine on stability operations. It provides more extensive discussions than JP 3-0 RAD on the principles and capabilities required when planning and conducting stability operations during major operations. *Military Support to Stabilization, Security, Transition, and Reconstruction Operations Joint Operating Concept,* version 1.9, has further advanced the concept.

b. The Army's stability operations construct characterized as a grouping of several types of operations (e.g., Peace Operations, Noncombatant Evacuation Operations) with common purposes and considerations is not consistent with DOD policy and joint doctrine; however, their construct was developed before and without the benefit of that guidance. Nevertheless, **many of the planning and other considerations addressed extensively in FM 3-07 could apply to the joint view of stability operations**.

c. Military support to SSTR operations is a CJCS JPME SAE. SAEs help ensure the currency and relevance of the colleges' JPME curricula and provide an independent view of what those curricula should address.

6. **Transnational criminal activities that support or sustain IW and the law enforcement activities to counter them** are unclear from the IW roadmap. Historically, US military forces generally do not conduct or support law enforcement activities, other than where specific authorities exist such as antipiracy, Military Support for Civil Law Enforcement Activities, and Counterdrug support. Currently US military forces

provide security during operations across the range of military operations.

7. **Civil-Military Operations.** CMO are well established and documented in joint doctrine. JP 3-57 is the dedicated publication on that subject. A joint working group was held 2-3 August 2006, hosted by USSOCOM, to review and refine the proposed program directive (PD) for JP 3-57, into the PD final coordination draft. The publication will consolidate JP 3-57 and JP 3-57.1, *Joint Doctrine for Civil Affairs.*

8. **Psychological Operations.** PSYOP are well established and documented in joint doctrine. JP 3-53 is the dedicated publication on that subject. The July 2005 preliminary assessment recommended an early formal assessment of the publication which is currently underway. Initial indications are that the publication should be revised on a normal schedule.

9. **Information Operations.** IO are well established and documented in joint doctrine. JP 3-13 is the dedicated publication on that subject and was revised in February 2006. The core capabilities of IO will be documented in a subordinate hierarchy under the 3-13 series of publications once those publications are revised. A preliminary assessment of this publication is scheduled to occur between August 2007 and February 2008.

10. **Intelligence and Counterintelligence Operations.** Intelligence and CI operations are well established and documented in joint doctrine with a dedicated keystone publication JP 2-0, a dedicated CI publication JP 2-01.2 *Counterintelligence and Human Intelligence Support to Joint Operations (U)*, and an associated hierarchy on joint intelligence. JP 2-0 is currently under revision with a revision first draft scheduled to be completed July 2006. JP 2-01.2 is classified publication (SECRET//NOFORN) under fast track revision and scheduled to be completed June 2006.

SECTION D. TERMS AND DEFINITIONS

This section analyzes terms and definitions to illustrate consistency or inconsistency of the definitions throughout DOD Directives, CJCS instructions, and joint doctrine.

1. **Conflict.** There are striking similarities between the DOD definition of conflict and the working definition of IW. In both definitions, the objectives are political, the indirect approach is employed, and the

military is used to support other capabilities or instruments of national power.

2. **Military Options.** Military options, as currently defined, include 5 of the 10 IW activities (aspects), e.g., civil affairs; PSYOP; support for law enforcement authorities to counter international criminal activities; terrorism and COIN; and civil war in foreign countries [FID]. Military options as a term is similar to, but inconsistent with, the range of military operations as discussed in JP 3-0 RAD.

3. **Stability Operations**. The definitions of stability operations in DODD 3000.05 and JP 3-0 RAD are different, but not inconsistent. The DODD 3000.05 definition includes military and civilian activities with a broad purpose, while the JP 3-0 RAD definition is limited to military activities outside the US in coordination with civilians for specified purposes.

4. **Military support to Stability, Security, Transition, and Reconstruction**. Although defined in DODD 3000.05, neither "SSTR" nor "SSTR operations" are defined in joint doctrine.

SECTION E. ADDITIONAL ANALYSIS

This section is provided to document other issues uncovered during research of IW.

1. CJCS JPME SAEs include CIST, which is not mentioned in policy or joint doctrine. While doctrine is the foundation of JPME, CIST is not described in doctrine, nor is there an approved concept describing CIST.

2. Research did not reveal IW in any treaties, international agreements, or other legal documents.

CHAPTER IV

CONCLUSIONS

> *"Gen. William Wallace said Unified Quest accomplished its goal of clarifying what irregular warfare really is. But he shied away from a rigid definition of such conflict, preferring to see the challenge as adjusting the mix of offensive, defensive, and stability operations to an ever changing environment. The key difference in these types of wars, he says, is that "people and culture and their aspirations are part of the terrain."."*
>
> U.S. News & World Report
> 8 May 2006

1. **Overview**. This chapter provides conclusions concerning doctrinal implications of IW as introduced/described in the 2006 QDR report and the subsequent IW roadmap. Specifically this chapter draws conclusions regarding the joint doctrinal treatment of IW; identifies joint doctrinal voids; and draws conclusions regarding terminology implications/ doctrinal issues related to IW. Additional conclusions are made regarding other doctrinal issues uncovered during research and analysis of IW.

2. **IW Construct and Definition.** IW is an undeveloped concept with an imprecise working definition. IW has no underlying principles. There is no policy on IW.

    a. IW is akin to well intentioned concepts such as "dominant maneuver" which do not transition into joint doctrine. While the character of warfare may change, its nature remains constant.

    b. IW is too broad a term to generate consensus as to its meaning.

    c. IW does not have potential doctrinal utility — there would be no value added to the warfighter to address IW in joint doctrine.

    d. **As a practical matter, the IW concept and descriptions available are too immature to develop a joint doctrine construct now and the potential for future development is doubtful based on the analysis presented in this study.**

3. **Activities of IW.** This paragraph states conclusions regarding the joint doctrinal treatment of each of the 10 IW activities (aspects) as listed in the IW roadmap.

a. **Insurgency and Counterinsurgency. There is a joint doctrinal void regarding COIN.** There is no operational level authoritative guidance for GPF to conduct long-duration COIN operations.

b. **Terrorism and Counterterrorism. There is a joint doctrinal void regarding CT.** There is no operational level authoritative guidance for GPF to conduct long-duration CT operations. **There is a joint doctrinal void regarding CbT.** While three of four actions of CbT are discussed in joint doctrine, they are fragmented and there is no overarching operational level authoritative guidance.

c. **Unconventional Warfare.** There is no doctrinal void regarding UW. A **doctrinal implication** of the 2006 QDR and IW roadmap **is the lack of** operational level authoritative **guidance for joint special operations support to conventional forces**.

d. **Foreign Internal Defense.** There is no doctrinal void regarding FID. A **doctrinal implication** of the 2006 QDR and IW roadmap is the **sparse** operational level authoritative **guidance for GPF to conduct FID**. Another **doctrinal implication is the lack** of operational level authoritative **guidance for GPF to train, equip, and advise large numbers of foreign security forces**.

e. **Stability, Security, Transition, and Reconstruction Operations**. The current doctrinal void regarding military support to SSTR operations will be filled upon approval of the JP 3-0 RAD (projected for the summer of 2006). The new joint doctrine on stability operations will provide basic guidance for military support to SSTR operations. Other proposed and approved guidance on stability operations in the joint operating concept and Army doctrine **should be considered for incorporation in future joint doctrine** should the joint doctrine development community demand more than JP 3-0 will deliver.

f. **Transnational criminal activities that support or sustain IW and the law enforcement activities to counter them.** While there is no operational level authoritative guidance for GPF to conduct activities that relate to this subject, none is required.

g. **Civil-Military Operations.** There is no doctrinal void regarding CMO. The 2006 QDR and IW roadmap do not introduce any doctrinal implications for CMO.

h. **Psychological Operations.** There is no doctrinal void regarding PSYOP. The 2006 QDR and IW roadmap do not introduce any doctrinal implications for PSYOP.

i. **Information Operations.** There are no doctrinal voids regarding IO. The 2006 QDR and IW roadmap do not introduce any doctrinal implications for IO.

j. **Intelligence and Counterintelligence Operations.** There is no doctrinal void regarding intelligence and counterintelligence. The 2006 QDR and IW roadmap do not introduce any doctrinal implications for intelligence and counterintelligence.

4. **Terms and Definitions.** This paragraph states conclusions regarding the joint doctrine terminology implications related to IW.

a. **Conflict.** The definition of conflict is satisfactory in joint doctrine.

b. **Military Options.** Military options appears to be an **orphaned term in joint doctrine**.

c. **Stability Operations.** The definitions of stability operations in DODD 3000.05 and the JP 3-0 RAD are different, but not inconsistent.

d. **Military support to Stability, Security, Transition, and Reconstruction.** While SSTR is not defined in joint doctrine, it need not be, since stability operations are defined and currently the only identified military mission per DOD policy. The term "stability operations" serves as the term for "military support to SSTR operations" during any doctrinal discussion.

5. **Additional Analysis**

a. The JPME SAE for **CIST has no foundation** and the concept has not progressed beyond briefing slides.

b. IW may raise legal issues based on the working definition and concept.

CHAPTER V

RECOMMENDATIONS

> *"War is war and strategy is strategy. Strategically approached, there is only war and warfare. It does not matter whether a conflict is largely of a regular or an irregular character; Clausewitz's general theory of war and strategy applies equally to both. The threat or use of force is instrumental for political purposes. The kinds of warfare are of no relevance whatever to the authority of the general theory of strategy. In short, irregular warfare, waged by a range of irregular enemies, is governed by exactly the same lore as is regular warfare, viewed strategically."*
>
> Colin S. Gray
> IRREGULAR ENEMIES AND THE ESSENCE OF STRATEGY:
> CAN THE AMERICAN WAY OF WAR ADAPT?
> U.S. Army War College, Strategic Studies Institute

1. **Overview**. This chapter provides recommendations concerning the doctrinal implications of IW as introduced/described in the 2006 QDR report and the subsequent IW roadmap. **Specifically this study does not recommend addressing IW in joint doctrine.** It does, however propose courses of action for resolving identified joint doctrine voids; and recommends terminology changes related to IW. Additional recommendations are made regarding other doctrinal issues uncovered during research and analysis of IW.

2. **Irregular Warfare Construct and Definition. Reject addressing IW as a term or construct in joint doctrine. Do not define it or include it in JP 1-02 or any other joint publications.**

3. **Activities of Irregular Warfare.** This paragraph provides a recommended development/revision plan for each joint publication or joint doctrine void relating to each of the 10 IW activities (aspects) as listed in the IW roadmap.

    a. **Insurgency and Counterinsurgency**. Two courses of action are proposed.

       (1) USJFCOM assess the need for and develop and submit a **joint doctrine project proposal on COIN**. This is the recommended course of action.

(2) Unless there is clamor from "the field" suggesting an earlier approach, **USJFCOM should** focus on the adequacy of COIN operations guidance during the preliminary assessment of JP 3-0 (around February 2008) per CJCSI 5120.02, *Joint Doctrine Development System.* This is an alternative course of action.

b. **Terrorism and Counterterrorism.** Two courses of action are proposed.

(1) USJFCOM assess the need for and develop and submit a **joint doctrine project proposal on CT and CbT**. Consider as an option to change the title and scope of JP 3-07.2 to include CbT and CT. This is the recommended course of action.

(2) Continue the normal maintenance on doctrine regarding AT. During this maintenance phase, a discussion of the need for operational level authoritative guidance for CbT and CT should occur. This is an alternative course of action.

c. **Unconventional Warfare**. Two courses of action are proposed.

(1) Conduct an **early formal assessment of JP 3-05** prior to June 2008. Specifically assess the need for a discussion of operational level authoritative guidance for joint special operations support to conventional forces. USSOCOM should remain the lead agent. This is the recommended course of action.

(2) Continue the normal maintenance of JP 3-05. During this maintenance phase, a discussion of the need for operational level authoritative guidance for special operations support to conventional forces should occur. This is an alternative course of action.

d. **Foreign Internal Defense**. Two courses of action are proposed.

(1) Conduct an early **formal assessment of JP 3-07.1** prior to January 2008. Assess the need for a discussion of operational level authoritative guidance for GPF to conduct FID and to train, equip, and advise large numbers of foreign security forces. USSOCOM should remain the lead agent. This is the recommended course of action.

(2) Continue the normal maintenance of JP 3-07.1. During this maintenance phase, a discussion of the need for operational level authoritative guidance for GPF to conduct FID should occur. USSOCOM is the lead agent. The maintenance phase will determine if another lead agent should be assigned. This is an alternative course of action.

e. **Stability, Security, Transition, and Reconstruction Operations.** Two courses of action are proposed.

(1) USJFCOM develop and submit a **joint doctrine project proposal on stability operations** and military support to SSTR operations. This is the recommended course of action.

(2) Unless there is clamor from "the field" suggesting an earlier approach, USJFCOM should focus on the adequacy of stability operations guidance during the preliminary assessment of JP 3-0 (around February 2008) per CJCSI 5120.02, *Joint Doctrine Development System.* This is an alternative course of action.

f. **Transnational criminal activities that support or sustain IW and the law enforcement activities to counter them.** Determine through approved JP maintenance assessments if a void has in fact emerged.

g. **Civil-Military Operations.** Continue the normal maintenance on doctrine regarding CMO.

h. **Psychological Operations.** Continue the normal maintenance on doctrine regarding PSYOP.

i. **Information Operations.** Continue the normal maintenance on doctrine regarding IO.

j. **Intelligence and Counterintelligence Operations.** Continue the normal maintenance on doctrine regarding intelligence and CI.

4. **Terms and Definitions.** This paragraph states recommendations regarding the joint doctrinal terminology implications related to IW.

a. **Conflict.** No change is required to the definition of conflict in joint doctrine.

b. **Military Options.** Military options should be **revised to reflect the range of military operations or deleted from joint doctrine**.

c. **Stability Operations**. The definition in DODD 3000.05 should be **changed to match the joint definition**, when approved.

d. **Military Support to Stability, Security, Transition, and Reconstruction.** Consider defining this term in joint doctrine when the JOC is published.

5. **Additional Analysis**

    a. The CJCS JPME SAE for **CIST should be deleted** until a policy or concept is approved.

    b. The IW concept and working definition should undergo legal review.

6. **Summary**. This report provided study results, research, analysis, conclusions, and recommendations concerning doctrinal implications of IW as introduced/described in the 2006 QDR and the subsequent IW roadmap. Specifically this study identified the current joint doctrinal treatment of IW and its activities (aspects), to include content of ongoing revision efforts; identified joint doctrinal voids concerning IW and proposes courses of action for resolving identified voids; and identified terminology implications/doctrinal issues related to IW.

REQUEST FOR IRREGULAR WARFARE STUDY

THE JOINT STAFF
WASHINGTON, DC

Reply ZIP Code: JUN 5 2006
20318-7000

MEMORANDUM FOR COMMANDER USJFCOM JOINT WARFIGHTING
                          CENTER

Subject: Request for Irregular Warfare Special Study

1. As agreed upon at the 37th Joint Doctrine Working Party, USJFCOM Joint Warfighting Center (JWFC) will research, analyze, and provide recommendations with respect to the doctrinal implications of Irregular Warfare (IW) as contained in the 2006 Quadrennial Defense Review (QDR) and the subsequent IW Roadmap. Specifically, this study should:

   a. Identify current joint doctrinal treatment of IW and its aspects, to include content of ongoing revision efforts.

   b. Identify joint doctrinal voids concerning IW. Propose courses of action for resolving identified voids, including recommendations for lead agency and timelines for resolution.

   c. Identify IW terminology implications/doctrinal issues.

2. Submit the study NLT 4 August 2006. Provide a 30-day update by 1 July 2006.

3. J-7 point of contact for this project is Col(s) Brent Goddard, DSN 222-6303, email: Brent.Goddard@js.pentagon.mil.

RICHARD J. MAULDIN
Rear Admiral, USN
Director for Operational Plans
and Joint Force Development

Copy to:
   JEDD

ENCLOSURE A

REQUEST FOR IRREGULAR WARFARE STUDY

Intentionally Blank

ENCLOSURE B

INSURGENCY AND COUNTERINSURGENCY

1. Insurgency and COIN are established terms in joint doctrine. While these terms appear in over 30 joint publications, there is almost no specific discussion in joint doctrine regarding them. Many joint publications that mention COIN refer back to FID, and while COIN is most frequently mentioned in FID, there is little discussion of specifics.

2. The following definitions of insurgency and counterinsurgency and related terms appear in joint doctrine:

counterinsurgency. Those military, paramilitary, political, economic, psychological, and civic actions taken by a government to defeat insurgency. Also called COIN. (JP 1-02)

insurgency. An organized movement aimed at the overthrow of a constituted government through use of subversion and armed conflict. (JP 1-02)

unconventional warfare. A broad spectrum of military and paramilitary operations, normally of long duration, predominantly conducted through, with, or by indigenous or surrogate forces who are organized, trained, equipped, supported, and directed in varying degrees by an external source. It includes, but is not limited to, guerrilla warfare, subversion, sabotage, intelligence activities, and unconventional assisted recovery. Also called UW. (JP 1-02)

counterguerrilla warfare. Operations and activities conducted by armed forces, paramilitary forces, or nonmilitary agencies against guerrillas. (JP 1-02)

guerrilla warfare. Military and paramilitary operations conducted in enemy-held or hostile territory by irregular, predominantly indigenous forces. Also called GW. See also unconventional warfare. (JP-3-05)

irregular forces. Armed individuals or groups who are not members of the regular armed forces, police, or other internal security forces. (JP 1-02)

guerrilla force. A group of irregular, predominantly indigenous personnel organized along military lines to conduct military and paramilitary operations in enemy-held, hostile, or denied territory. (JP 1-02)

3. There are eight Universal Joint Tasks associated with COIN:

   a. SN 8.1 Support Other Nations or Groups

   b. ST 2.1.1 Determine and Prioritize Theater Strategic Priority Intelligence Requirements (PIR)

   c. ST 3.2.2 Conduct Attack on Theater Strategic Targets/Target Systems Using Nonlethal Means

   d. ST 7.1.6 Determine Theater Force Size and Structure Requirements

   e. ST 8 Develop and Maintain Alliance and Regional Relations

   f. ST 8.2.9 Coordinate Theater Foreign Internal Defense Activities

   g. OP 2.1.1 Determine and Prioritize Operational Priority Intelligence Requirements (PIR)

   h. OP 3.1 Conduct Joint Force Targeting

ENCLOSURE C

TERRORISM AND COUNTERTERRORISM

1. Terrorism and counterterrorism (CT) are established terms in joint doctrine. CT is mentioned in over 35 JPs. CT is one of four actions of combating terrorism — AT (defensive measures used to reduce the vulnerability to terrorist acts), CT (offensive measures taken to prevent, deter, preempt, and respond to terrorism), CM (preparation for and response to consequences of a terrorist incident), and intelligence support (collection or dissemination of terrorism-related information). These four actions are taken to oppose terrorism throughout the entire threat spectrum. CT is one of nine core tasks SOF are specifically organized, trained, and equipped to accomplish. DOD plays an important role in domestic CT support to the FBI. Although frequently mentioned in joint doctrine, there is sparse discussion of CT in unclassified JPs.

2. The following definitions of terrorism and CT and related terms appear in joint doctrine:

> **counterterrorism.** Operations that include the offensive measures taken to prevent, deter, preempt, and respond to terrorism. Also called CT. (JP 3-05)

> **combating terrorism.** Actions, including antiterrorism (defensive measures taken to reduce vulnerability to terrorist acts) and counterterrorism (offensive measures taken to prevent, deter, and respond to terrorism), taken to oppose terrorism throughout the entire threat spectrum. Also called CbT. (JP 3-07.2)

> **military support to civilian law enforcement agencies.** A mission of civil support that includes support to civilian law enforcement agencies. This includes but is not limited to: combating terrorism, counterdrug operations, national security special events, and national critical infrastructure and key asset protection. Also called MSCLEA.

> **nation assistance.** Civil and/or military assistance rendered to a nation by foreign forces within that nation's territory during peacetime, crises or emergencies, or war based on agreements mutually concluded between nations. Nation assistance programs include, but are not limited to, security assistance, foreign internal defense, other US Code title 10 (DOD) programs, and activities performed on a

reimbursable basis by Federal agencies or intergovernmental organizations.

narco-terrorism. Terrorism conducted to further the aims of drug traffickers. It may include assassinations, extortion, hijackings, bombings, and kidnappings directed against judges, prosecutors, elected officials, or law enforcement agents, and general disruption of a legitimate government to divert attention from drug operations. (JP 3-07.4)

terrorism. The calculated use of unlawful violence or threat of unlawful violence to inculcate fear; intended to coerce or to intimidate governments or societies in the pursuit of goals that are generally political, religious, or ideological. (JP 3-07.2)

3. There is one Universal Joint Task associated with CT:

SN 8.1.10 Coordinate Actions to Combat Terrorism

ENCLOSURE D

UNCONVENTIONAL WARFARE

1. Unconventional warfare (UW) is an established term in joint doctrine, referred to in 35 JPs and, defined as:

> *"A broad spectrum of military and paramilitary operations, normally of long duration, predominantly conducted through, with, or by indigenous or surrogate forces who are organized, trained, equipped, supported and directed in varying degrees by an external source. It includes, but is not limited to, guerrilla warfare, subversion, sabotage, intelligence activities, and unconventional assisted recovery. (JP 1-02)"*

A search of joint doctrine publications and resources for UW returned over 220 references in over 25 JPs. UW is primarily discussed in JP 3-05, *Doctrine for Joint Special Operations.* UW is unique in that it is special operations that can either be conducted as part of a geographic combatant commander's overall theater campaign, or as an independent, subordinate campaign. When conducted independently, the primary focus of UW is on political-military objectives and psychological objectives. UW includes military and paramilitary aspects of resistance movements. UW military activity represents the culmination of a successful effort to organize and mobilize the civil populace against a hostile government or occupying power. From the US perspective, the intent is to develop and sustain these supported resistance organizations and to synchronize their activities to further US national security objectives. SOF units do not create resistance movements. They advise, train, and assist indigenous resistance movements already in existence to conduct UW and when required, accompany them into combat. When UW operations support conventional military operations, the focus shifts to primarily military objectives; however the political and psychological implications remain. Operational and strategic staffs and commanders must guard against limiting UW to a specific set of circumstances or activities defined by either recent events or personal experience. The most prevalent mistake is the belief that UW is limited to guerrilla warfare or insurgency.

2. UW includes, but is not limited to, the following activities:

   a. **Guerrilla Warfare.** These are military and paramilitary operations conducted by irregular, predominantly indigenous forces in adversary-held or hostile territory. It is the military aspect of an insurgency or other armed resistance movement. Guerilla warfare techniques can undermine the legitimacy of the existing government or an occupying power as well as destroy, degrade, or divert military capabilities.

b. **Subversion.** These operations are designed to undermine the military, economic, psychological, or political strength or morale of a regime or nation. The clandestine nature of subversion dictates that the underground elements perform the bulk of the activity.

c. **Sabotage.** These are operations that involve an act or acts with intent to injure, interfere with, or obstruct the national defense of a country by willfully injuring or destroying, or attempting to injure or destroy, any national defense or war material, premises, or utilities, to include human and natural resources. Sabotage selectively disrupts, destroys, or neutralizes hostile capabilities with a minimum expenditure of manpower and materiel.

d. **Intelligence Activities.** These activities assess areas of interest ranging from political and military personalities to the military capabilities of friendly and adversary forces. SOF perform intelligence activities ranging from developing information critical to planning and conducting operations, to assessing the capabilities and intentions of indigenous and coalition forces.

e. **Unconventional Assisted Recovery (UAR).** These operations consist of UW forces establishing and operating unconventional assisted recovery mechanisms and unconventional assisted recovery teams. UAR operations are designed to seek out, contact, authenticate, and support military and other selected personnel as they move from an adversary-held, hostile, or sensitive area to areas under friendly control.

3. NATO doctrine addresses unconventional warfare with this definition:

> "**unconventional warfare.** *General term used to describe operations conducted for military, political or economic purposes within an area occupied by the enemy and making use of the local inhabitants and resources. (AAP-6, NATO Glossary of Terms and Definitions, 2006)*"

4. There are three Universal Joint Tasks associated with unconventional warfare:

a. ST 1.3.7 Conduct Unconventional Warfare (UW) Across Joint Operations Areas

b. ST 3.2.1 Conduct Attack on Theater Strategic Targets/Target Systems Using Lethal Means

c. OP 1.2.4.8 Conduct Unconventional Warfare in the Joint Operations Area

ENCLOSURE E

FOREIGN INTERNAL DEFENSE

1. Foreign internal defense (FID) is a well established program defined in JP 3-07.1, *Joint Tactics, Techniques, and Procedures for Foreign Internal Defense (FID),* as "the participation by civilian and military agencies of a government in any of the action programs taken by another government or other designated organization, to free and protect its society from subversion, lawlessness, and insurgency." A search of joint doctrine publications and resources for FID returned over 700 references in over 30 JPs.

2. FID seeks to enhance the credibility and legitimacy of the "relevant political authority. The focus of all US foreign internal defense (FID) efforts is to support the host nation's (HN's) program of internal defense and development (IDAD). These national programs are designed to free and protect a nation from subversion, lawlessness, and insurgency by emphasizing the building of viable institutions that respond to the needs of society. The most significant manifestation of these needs is likely to be economic, social, informational, or political; therefore, these needs should prescribe the principal focus of US efforts. The United States will generally employ a mix of diplomatic, economic, informational, and military instruments of national power in support of these objectives. Programs may include multinational exercises, exchange programs, civil-military operations, intelligence and communications sharing, logistic support of security assistance, and combat operations. Military assistance is often necessary in order to provide the secure environment for the above efforts to become effective."

3. FID supports three Universal Joint Tasks:

    a. SN 8.1.8 Provide Support to Foreign Internal Defense in Theater

    b. ST 8.2.9 Coordinate Theater Foreign Internal Defense Activities

    c. OP 4.7.7 Conduct Foreign Internal Defense (FID)

ENCLOSURE F

**STABILITY, SECURUITY, TRANSTION, AND
RECONSTRUCTION OPERATIONS**

1. The IW roadmap describes SSTR operations as "operations conducted to set conditions for the establishment or restoration of order and to enable the transition of governmental and security functions to legitimate, and preferably indigenous, civil authorities. **In SSTR operations, the principal role of U.S. military forces is to set security conditions**."

2. Department of Defense Directive (DODD) 3500.05, *Military Support for Stability, Security, Transition, and Reconstruction (SSTR) Operations*, November 2005, provides the following definitions:

    a. **Stability Operations.** Military and civilian activities conducted across the spectrum from peace to conflict to establish or maintain order in States and regions.

    b. **Military support to Stability, Security, Transition and Reconstruction (SSTR).** Department of Defense activities that support US Government plans for stabilization, security, reconstruction and transition operations, which lead to sustainable peace while advancing US interests.

3. Joint Publication (JP) 3-0 RAD, *Joint Operations*, establishes basic joint doctrine for stability operations. Key points include:

    a. **Stability Operations** is defined as an "overarching term encompassing various military missions, tasks, and activities conducted outside the United States in coordination with other instruments of national power to maintain or re-establish a safe and secure environment, provide essential governmental services, emergency infrastructure reconstruction, and humanitarian relief as required."

    b. Stability operations are planned and/or conducted and integrated with offensive and defensive operations in all joint operation phases, but are most prevalent in the latter phases. An example is the shift of focus from sustained combat operations in the "dominate" phase to a preponderance of stability operations in the "stabilize" and "enable civil authority" phases (Figure F-1).

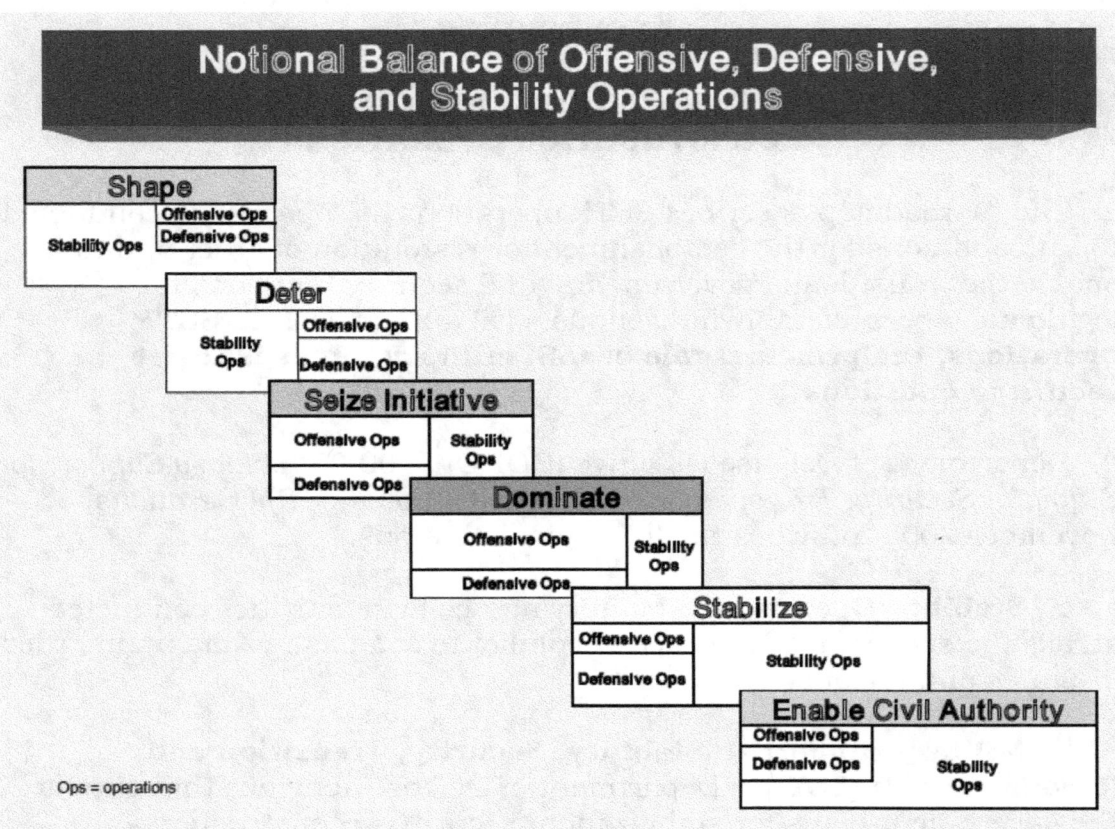

Figure F-1. Notional Balance of Offensive, Defensive, and Stability Operations

4. The *Stability Operations Joint Operating Concept* was published in September 2004. This joint operating concept posits an operational level solution for a very challenging future military problem: how the Joint Force can more effectively prepare for and conduct stabilization, security, transition and reconstruction operations to assist governments or regions under serious stress. Additionally, this JOC identifies the operational capabilities required for achieving military campaign objectives and effects in support of national strategic end-states. The *Military Support to Stabilization, Security, Transition, and Reconstruction Operations Joint Operating Concept* version 1.9 as of 22 June 2006 is currently being revised and staffed by USJFCOM J9 and will replace the 2004 *Stability Operations Joint Operating Concept.*

5. NATO and Army doctrine do not conform to the latest policy and joint doctrine. A more detailed examination is not considered relevant to this portion of the study.

6. There are no Universal Joint Tasks associated with stability operations.

7. There are three Universal Joint Tasks associated with stability:

   a. ST 5.2.4, Review International Security Considerations.

   b. ST 8.1, Coordinate Coalitions or Alliances, Regional Relations and Security Assistance Activities.

   c. OP 5.3.3, Determine Operational End State.

8. There are 14 OP and ST tasks associated with security as follows:

   a. ST 2.4.1.1, Identify Theater Issues and Threats.

   b. ST 4.2.3, Reconstitute Theater Forces.

   c. ST 5, Provide Theater Strategic Command and Control, Communications, and Computers (C4).

   d. ST 5.1, Operate and Manage Theater C4I Environment.

   e. ST 5.1.1.1, Manage a Theater Communications Security (COMSEC) Management Branch.

   f. ST 5.2, Assess Theater Strategic Environment.

   g. ST 5.2.3, Review National Security Considerations.

   h. ST 5.2.4, Review International Security Considerations.

   i. ST 5.3.1.4, Conduct Mission Analysis and Prepare Mission Statement.

   j. ST 5.5, Conduct Theater-Wide Information Operations (IO).

   k. ST 5.5.1, Plan and Integrate Theater-Wide Information Operation (IO).

   j. ST 5.5.3, Establish and Monitor Theater Information Security Policy, Plans, Programs, and Direction.

   k. OP 2.2, Collect and Share Operational Information.

   l. OP 2.4.1.1, Identify Operational Issues and Threats.

m. OP 4.7, Provide Politico-Military Support to Other Nations, Groups, and Government Agencies.

n. OP 4.7.1, Provide Security Assistance in the Joint Operations Area.

ENCLOSURE G

TRANSNATIONAL CRIMINAL ACTIVITIES THAT SUPPORT OR SUSTAIN IRREGULAR WARFARE AND THE LAW ENFORCEMENT ACTIVITIES TO COUNTER THEM

1. Transnational criminal activities that support or sustain IW and the law enforcement activities to counter them are not defined nor specifically discussed in joint doctrine. Indirectly, these activities fall under the areas of CI and international terrorism.

2. The following JPs discuss CI and international terrorism activities:

   a. JP 2-01, *Joint and National Intelligence Support to Military Operations,* states the FBI Foreign Counterintelligence and International Terrorism Program is responsible for:

   (1) Conducting CI activities within the US.

   (2) Conducting CI activities outside the US in coordination with the Central Intelligence Agency, as required by agreement of the Director for Central Intelligence and the Attorney General.

   (3) Collecting, producing, and disseminating foreign intelligence and CI.

   (4) Carrying out research, development, and procurement of technical systems and devices related to their authorized functions.

   b. JP 2-01.2, *Joint Tactics, Techniques, and Procedures for Counterintelligence Support to Operations,* states that the following agencies are responsible for international crime activities:

   (1) Federal Bureau of Investigation. Under the authority of Executive Order 12333, *United States Intelligence Activities,* the FBI's Counterintelligence and Counterterrorism Divisions conduct and coordinate CI and CT activities, respectively, within the United States. The CI division conducts and coordinates espionage investigations and other CI investigations. The CI Division detects and counteracts foreign threats to the US Government (USG) and US corporations, establishments, or persons, and collects CI and foreign intelligence information. The CT Division combats domestic and international terrorism and works closely with the CI Division in countering threats to the USG, US corporations, establishments, or persons, while collecting information concerning both domestic and international terrorism.

(2) Drug Enforcement Administration (DEA). The DEA enforces laws and regulations governing narcotics and controlled substances, chemical diversion, and trafficking. DEA is also the lead agency for overseas for counterdrug law enforcement activities and investigations. DEA contributes to intelligence as a byproduct of efforts to build legal cases against narcotics traffickers. Since drug trafficking is often connected to international terrorism, DEA agents often operate within combatant command operational areas. DEA-collected and produced information is potentially valuable in DOD CT operations.

3. There are twelve Universal Joint Tasks associated with terrorist activities:

a. SN 3.4.7 Coordinate Force Protection for Strategic Forces and Means

b. SN 3.4.7.1 Produce Counter Terrorism Intelligence

c. SN 8.1 Support Other Nations or Groups

d. SN 8.1.10 Coordinate Actions to Combat Terrorism

e. SN 8.2.2 Support Other Government Agencies

f. SN 9.4 Support WMD Nonproliferation and Counterproliferation Activities and Programs

g. ST 7.1.6 Determine Theater Force Size and Structure Requirements

h. ST 8 Develop and Maintain Alliance and Regional Relations

i. ST 8.3.4 Obtain Multinational Support Against Nonmilitary Threats

j. ST 8.4 Provide Theater Support to Other DOD and Government Agencies

k. ST 8.4.2 Combat Terrorism

l. OP 6.5 Provide Security for Operational Forces and Means

ENCLOSURE H

CIVIL-MILITARY OPERATIONS

1. Civil-Military Operations (CMO) are discussed throughout current joint publications and associated documents. A search of joint doctrine publications and resources for CMO resulted in locating over 850 references in over 20 JPs. JP 3-57, *Joint Doctrine for Civil-Military Operations,* provides the flowing definition for Civil-Military Operations:

> *"The activities of a commander that establish, maintain, influence, or exploit relations between forces, governmental and nongovernmental civilian organizations and authorities, and the civilian populace in a friendly, neutral, or hostile operational area in order to facilitate military operations, to consolidate and achieve operational US objectives. Civil-military operations may include performance by military forces of activities and functions normally the responsibility of the local, regional, or national government. These activities may occur prior to, during, or subsequent to other military actions. They may also occur, if directed, in the absence of other military operations. Civil-military operations may be performed by designated civil affairs, by other military forces, or by a combination of civil affairs and other forces."*

2. CMO is not exclusive to IW and is planned for and used in virtually all types of US military campaigns and operations. "CMO are conducted to minimize civilian interference with military operations, to maximize support for operations...CMO are conducted across the range of military operations to address root causes of instability and in a reconstructive manner after conflict or disaster, or may be conducted in mitigating circumstances to support US national security objectives. CMO may also include psychological operations and [civil affairs] CA activities." (JP 3-57)

3. There are five Universal Joint Tasks associated with CMO:

    a. SN 8.1 Support Other Nations or Groups

    b. ST 8.2 Provide Support to Allies, Regional Governments, International Organizations or Groups

    c. OP 4.7 Provide Politico-Military Support to Other Nations, Groups, and Government Agencies

    d. OP 4.7.2 Conduct Civil Military Operations in the Joint Operations Area

e. OP 4.7.7 Conduct Foreign Internal Defense (FID)

ENCLOSURE I

PSYCHOLOGICAL OPERATIONS

1. Psychological Operations (PSYOP) is integrated throughout JPs and associated documents. A search of the JEL resulted in locating over 300 references to PSYOP in 41 joint publications. PSYOP are defined as:

> *"Planned operations to convey selected information and indicators to foreign audiences to influence their emotions, motives, objective reasoning, and ultimately the behavior of foreign governments, organizations, groups, and individuals. The purpose of psychological operations is to induce or reinforce foreign attitudes and behavior favorable to the originator's objectives. Also called PSYOP. (JP 1-02)"*

JP 3-53, *Joint Doctrine for Psychological Operations*, addresses military psychological operations planning and execution in support of joint, multinational, and interagency efforts across the range of military operations. "PSYOP are a vital part of the broad range of US diplomatic, informational, military, and economic activities. PSYOP characteristically are delivered as information for effect, used during peacetime and conflict, to inform and influence." (JP 3-53)

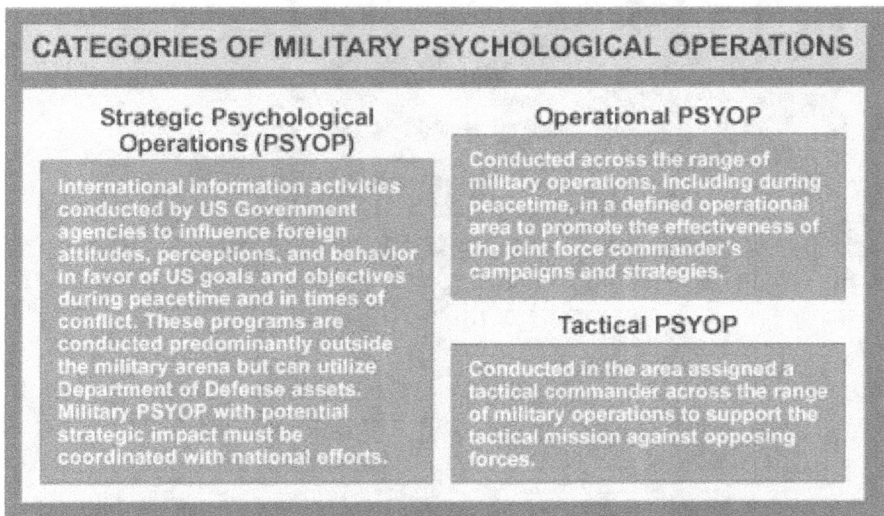

Figure I-1. Categories of Military Psychological Operations

"PSYOP applicability to the range of military operations [figure below] describes each in discrete terms, in actual circumstance there may not be a precise boundary where a particular state ends and another begins." (JP 3-53)

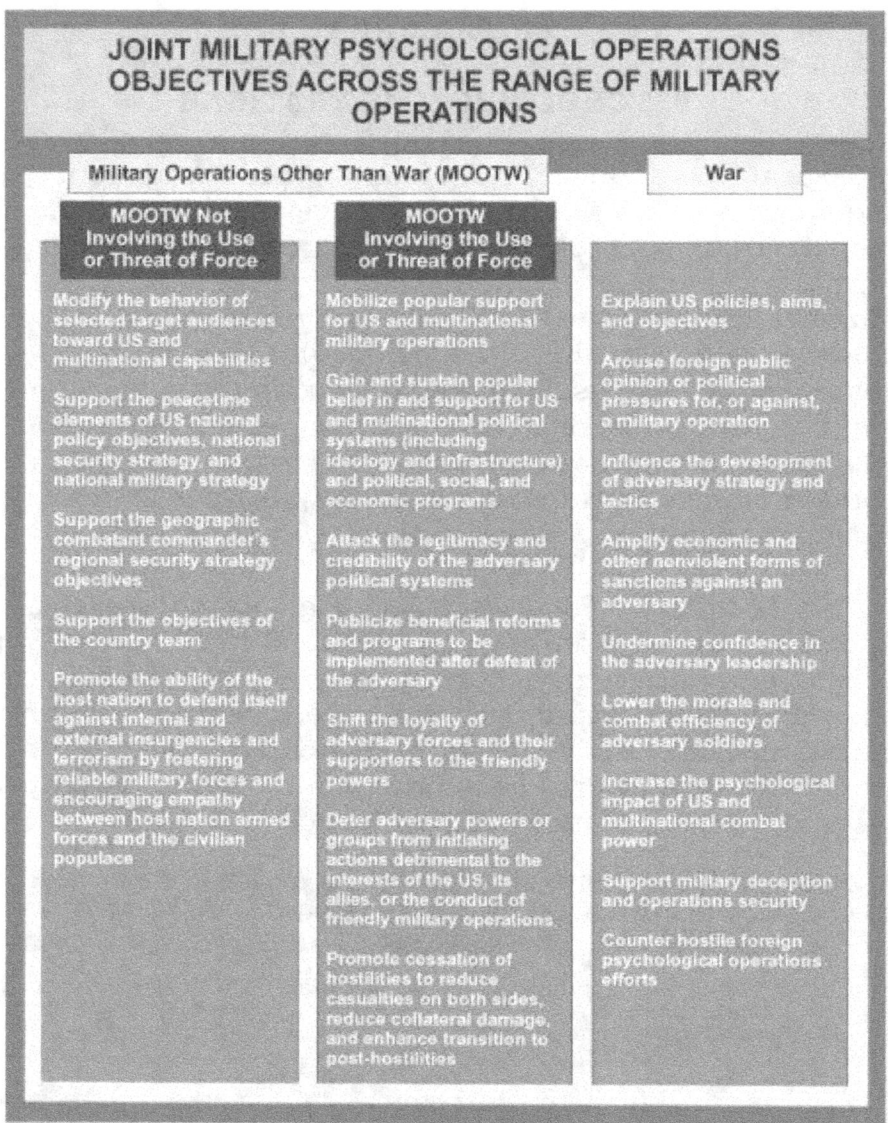

JOINT MILITARY PSYCHOLOGICAL OPERATIONS OBJECTIVES ACROSS THE RANGE OF MILITARY OPERATIONS

Military Operations Other Than War (MOOTW)		War
MOOTW Not Involving the Use or Threat of Force	**MOOTW Involving the Use or Threat of Force**	
Modify the behavior of selected target audiences toward US and multinational capabilities	Mobilize popular support for US and multinational military operations	Explain US policies, aims, and objectives
Support the peacetime elements of US national policy objectives, national security strategy, and national military strategy	Gain and sustain popular belief in and support for US and multinational political systems (including ideology and infrastructure) and political, social, and economic programs	Arouse foreign public opinion or political pressures for, or against, a military operation
Support the geographic combatant commander's regional security strategy objectives	Attack the legitimacy and credibility of the adversary political systems	Influence the development of adversary strategy and tactics
Support the objectives of the country team	Publicize beneficial reforms and programs to be implemented after defeat of the adversary	Amplify economic and other nonviolent forms of sanctions against an adversary
Promote the ability of the host nation to defend itself against internal and external insurgencies and terrorism by fostering reliable military forces and encouraging empathy between host nation armed forces and the civilian populace	Shift the loyalty of adversary forces and their supporters to the friendly powers	Undermine confidence in the adversary leadership
	Deter adversary powers or groups from initiating actions detrimental to the interests of the US, its allies, or the conduct of friendly military operations	Lower the morale and combat efficiency of adversary soldiers
	Promote cessation of hostilities to reduce casualties on both sides, reduce collateral damage, and enhance transition to post-hostilities	Increase the psychological impact of US and multinational combat power
		Support military deception and operations security
		Counter hostile foreign psychological operations efforts

Figure I-2. Joint Military Psychological Operations Objective Across the Range of Military Operations

Military Operations Other Than War (MOOTW) is a term that is being deleted from joint lexicon. No one-for-one replacement term has been identified. In any event PSYOP span the range of military operations.

"As one of the core capabilities of information operations (IO), psychological operations (PSYOP) must be integrated with the other IO capabilities providing mutual benefits for both. PSYOP are used to conduct counterpropaganda, induce or reinforce attitudes and behavior to friendly objectives, and discourage support for adversaries and their goals." (JP 3-53)

2. Chairman of the Joint Chiefs of Staff Instruction (CJSCI) 3110.05C, *Joint Psychological Operations Supplement to the Joint Strategic Capabilities Plan FY 2002*, 18 July 2003, states "PSYOP forces provide the President, Secretary of Defense, combatant commanders, JFCs, and when directed, chiefs of US diplomatic missions with a unique tool to support peacetime activities, contingency operations, and declared war."

3. NATO PSYOPS Policy MC 402 (17 April 2003) defines PSYOPS as: "Planned psychological activities using methods of communications and other means directed to approved audiences in order to influence perceptions, attitudes and behaviour, affecting the achievement of political and military objectives." Whilst some Allied countries differ in their national definitions of PSYOPS, all have agreed to the definition contained in MC 402, on which this AJP is founded. (AJP-3.10.1 Allied Joint Doctrine for Psychological Operations, 2d Study Draft, 1 April 2006)

"NATO has no standing PSYOPS forces; the only permanent PSYOPS capability currently under NATO command is the presence of staff officers with PSYOPS responsibilities within the peacetime organisation at SC, JFC and JFC component levels." (AJP-3.10.1 Allied Joint Doctrine for Psychological Operations, 2d Study Draft, 1 April 2006)

"Member Nations are responsible for developing plans and programmes in support of NATO PSYOPS policy and doctrine, for ensuring that interoperability with other NATO Nations is taken into consideration during development and procurement of national PSYOPS capabilities, for ensuring that, if appropriate and within national capabilities, intelligence, research, and analysis is provided in support of NATO PSYOPS, and for providing, where possible, national resources and trained personnel to support NATO PSYOPS in operations and exercises." (AJP-3.10.1 Allied Joint Doctrine for Psychological Operations, 2d Study Draft, 1 April 2006)

AJP-3.10.1 does provide doctrine for structuring and employing forces for combined joint psychological operations.

4. There are six Universal Joint Tasks associated with PSYOP:

  a. SN 5.5 Coordinate Worldwide Information

  b. ST 3.2.2 Conduct Attack on Theater Strategic Targets/Target Systems Using Nonlethal Means

  c. ST 3.2.2.1 Conduct Theater Psychological Activities

d. ST 5.5 Conduct Theater-Wide Information Operations (IO)

e. OP 3.2.2 Conduct Attack on Operational Targets Using Nonlethal Means

f. OP 3.2.2.1 Employ PSYOP in the Joint Operations Area.

ENCLOSURE J

INFORMATION OPERATIONS

1. Information Operations (IO) are integrated throughout JPs and associated documents. A search of the JEL resulted in locating 615 references to IO in 37 JPs. JP 3-13, *Information Operations*, provides doctrine for information operations planning, preparation, execution, and assessment in support of joint operations. IO is **defined as:**

> *"The integrated employment of the core capabilities of electronic warfare, computer network operations, psychological operations, military deception, and operations security, in concert with specified supporting and related capabilities, to influence, disrupt, corrupt or usurp adversarial human and automated decision making while protecting our own. Also called IO. (This term and its definition modify the existing term and its definition and are approved for inclusion in the next edition of JP 1-02.)"*

IO is not exclusive to IW. "IO capabilities can produce effects and achieve objectives at all levels of war and across the range of military operations. The nature of the modern information environment complicates the identification of the boundaries between these levels. Therefore, at all levels, information activities, including IO must be consistent with broader national security policy and strategic objectives." (JP 3-13)

"IO consists of five core capabilities which are: psychological operations (PSYOP), military deception (MILDEC), operations security (OPSEC), electronic warfare (EW), and computer network operations (CNO)...Together these five capabilities, used in conjunction with supporting and related capabilities, provide the [Joint Force Commander] JFC with the principal means of influencing an adversary and other target audiences (TAs)." (JP 3-13)

"Capabilities supporting IO include information assurance (IA), physical security, physical attack, counterintelligence, and combat camera." (JP 3-13)

"There are three military functions, public affairs (PA), civil military operations (CMO), and defense support to public diplomacy, specified as related capabilities for IO." (JP 3-13).

JP 3-13 does not reference IW but does reference irregular forces. "To apply IO across the range of military operations, the JFC integrates his military actions, forces, and capabilities throughout the domains (air, land, sea, and space) of the operating environment in order to create and/or sustain desired and measurable effects on adversary leaders, forces (regular or irregular), information, information systems, and other audiences." (JP3-13)

2. Chairman of the Joint Chiefs of Staff Instruction (CJCSI) 3210.01A, *Joint Information Operations Policy*, 6 November 1998 states "IO is one of many aspects of the US military's instruments of national power. DOD IO supports the overall US Government (USG) strategic engagement policy during peacetime, crisis, conflict, and post-conflict. IO is full spectrum strategies, which have applications that may be used during peacetime and across the range of military operations at every level of warfare. IO must be synchronized with air, land, sea, space, and special operations -- as well as interagency and multinational operations -- in harmony with diplomatic, economic, and efforts to attain national and multinational objectives.

3. The NATO policy for Info Ops [Information Operations] is under review. This review includes potential changes to the definition of Info Ops. [NATO] defines Info Ops as 'coordinated actions to create desired effects on the will, understanding and capability of adversaries, potential adversaries and other approved parties in support of Alliance overall objectives by affecting their information, information-based processes and systems while exploiting and protecting one's own.' (AJP-3.10 *Allied Joint Doctrine for Information Operations*, 4th Study Draft, January 2006)

"Activities coordinated through Info Ops ... focus directly on influencing will; affecting understanding and those capabilities that directly enable understanding or the application of will. They therefore have applicability across the range of military operations." (AJP-3.10 *Allied Joint Doctrine for Information Operations*, 4th Study Draft, January 2006)

The tools and techniques that form the basis of most Info Ops activity "include Psychological Operations (PSYOPS), presence posture and profile (PPP), OPSEC, Information Security (INFOSEC), deception, Electronic Warfare (EW), physical destruction and Computer Network Operations (CNO)." (AJP-3.10 *Allied Joint Doctrine for Information Operations*, 4th Study Draft, January 2006)

"Civil Military Cooperation (CIMIC) and [Public Information] (PI) are military capabilities that require Alliance direction and guidance separate and distinct from Info Ops. However, as they will always be part of the Alliance Info Strategy, they will require very close coordination with Info

Ops activity." (AJP-3.10 Allied Joint Doctrine for Information Operations, 4th Study Draft, January 2006)

4. There are 17 Universal Joint Tasks associated with IO:

   a. SN 3.2.5 Determine National Strategic Targeting Policy

   b. SN 3.2.6 Develop National Strategic Attack Policy

   c. SN 3.3.4 Apply National Nonlethal Capabilities

   d. SN 5.5 Coordinate Worldwide Information Operations

   e. SN 5.5.1 Conduct Strategic Information Operations

   f. SN 5.5.2 Conduct Defensive Information Operations

   g. SN 8.3.5 Coordinate DOD/Government Information Operations (IO)

   h. ST 1.3.4 Integrate Direct Action in Theater

   i. ST 1.6.4 Gain and Maintain Information Superiority in Theater

   j. ST 3.2.2 Conduct Attack on Theater Strategic Targets/Target Systems Using Nonlethal Means

   k. ST 5.5 Conduct Theater-Wide Information Operations (IO)

   l. ST 5.5.1 Plan and Integrate Theater-Wide Information Operation (IO)

   m. ST 5.5.2 Control Theater Information Operations (IO)

   n. ST 5.5.3 Establish and Monitor Theater Information Security Policy, Plans, Programs, and Direction

   o. OP 5.6 Coordinate Operational Information Operations (IO)

   p. OP 5.6.1 Integrate Operational Information Operations

   q. OP 5.6.3 Control Information Operations

ENCLOSURE K

INTELLIGENCE AND COUNTERINTELLIGENCE

1. Intelligence and counterintelligence (CI) are discussed throughout current joint publications and associated documents. A search of the JEL resulted in locating references to intelligence in 83 JPs and CI in 43 JPs.

    a. JP 2-0, *Doctrine for Intelligence Support to Joint Operations*, 09 March 2003, defines intelligence and CI.

> ***"intelligence.*** *1. The product resulting from the collection, processing, integration, analysis, evaluation, and interpretation of available information concerning foreign countries or areas. 2. Information and knowledge about an adversary obtained through observation, investigation, analysis, or understanding."*

> ***"counterintelligence.*** *Information gathered and activities conducted to protect against espionage, other intelligence activities, sabotage, or assassinations conducted by or on behalf of foreign governments or elements thereof, foreign organizations, or foreign persons, or international terrorist activities. Also called CI."*

    b. The following publications discuss intelligence operations and CI operations in relationship to terrorist activities:

    (1) JP 2-01, *Joint and National Intelligence Support to Military Operations*:

    (a) CI support is crucial to protecting the force and combating terrorism and must be fully integrated into operation planning and execution. The Department of Defense CI program has four separate but interrelated functions: investigations; collection; operations; and analysis and production. All four functions will be incorporated into CI planning and support activities. The Counterintelligence Field Activity (CIFA) and CI elements from the Service components play a lead role in this multidisciplined effort and facilitate information sharing among combatant commands, interagency partners, and law enforcement organizations.

    (b) Defense Intelligence Support Office (DISO). [Defense Intelligence Agency] DIA maintains DISOs at each of the combatant commands, US Forces Korea, and Supreme HQ Allied Powers Europe and North Atlantic Treaty Organization (NATO) HQ. Each DISO includes a senior DIA intelligence officer, who serves as chief of the DISO and as the personal representative of the DIA Director; an administrative assistant; and a varying number of DIA functional intelligence specialists based on the needs of the supported command. The typical DISO includes a [Human Intelligence] HUMINT support element (HSE), consisting of one or more [Defense Human Intelligence Service] DHS personnel; an intelligence production liaison officer; and a measurement and signatures intelligence liaison officer (MASLO). Some DISOs also have information technology and Joint Intelligence Task Force Combating Terrorism (JITF-CT) representatives.

(c) The Joint Intelligence Task Force — Combating Terrorism is a component of the Joint Staff J-2 and is responsible for directing collection, exploitation, analysis, and dissemination of all-source intelligence in support of DOD force protection, counterterrorism, and antiterrorism operations and planning. The JITF-CT also focuses on providing strategic and tactical warning exposing and exploiting terrorist vulnerabilities, and supporting operations to prevent terrorists and their sponsors from acquiring increased capabilities, particularly in the area of WMD.

(2) JP 2.01.3, *Joint Tactics, Techniques, and Procedures for Joint Intelligence Preparation of the Battlespace* (JIPB). This publication has a chapter (IV) on JIPB support to countering asymmetric warfare threats and a chapter on JIPB support to Military Operation Other Than War (MOOTW). [Note: MOOTW is being deleted from joint doctrine.]

(a) MOOTW operations include: arms control; combating terrorism; Department of Defense support to counterdrug operations; enforcement of sanctions/maritime intercept operations; enforcing exclusion zones; ensuring freedom of navigation and overflight; humanitarian assistance; military support to civil authorities; nation assistance/support to counterinsurgency; noncombatant evacuation operations; peace operations; protection of shipping; recovery operations; show of force operations; strikes and raids; and support to insurgency.

(b) Several types of joint force activities and operations are applicable to deterring or counter an adversary's use of asymmetric warfare. JIPB support to these types of joint force activities may require a slightly different focus.

(c) JIPB support to MOOTW must facilitate parallel planning by all strategic, operation, and tactical units involved in the operation.

(3) JP 3.07.2, *Antiterrorism* (AT), provides doctrine on how to organize, plan, train for, and conduct joint antiterrorism operations and interagency AT coordination. JP 3.07.2 has an entire chapter on intelligence, CI, threat analysis, and countersurveillance. It states that, intelligence and CI are critical in the development of an AT program. Strategic, well-planned, proactive, systematic, all-source intelligence, and CI programs are essential. The role of intelligence and CI is to identify, assess, deter, disrupt, and defeat the threat, provide advance warning, and disseminate critical information/intelligence in a usable form for the commander. It discusses how terrorist networks have twisted the benefits and conveniences of our increasingly open, integrated, and modernized world to serve their agenda. Various countries provided sanctuary for terrorist camps and certain bank accounts in these countries served as a trust fund for terrorism.

2. NATO doctrine address various aspects of intelligence. AJP-2.1(A), *Intelligence Procedures*, discusses Asymmetric Threats below.

a. With the end of the Cold War and changes in the strategic balance, the threat of high intensity conflict is diminished, making crisis response operations (CRO) among the more likely missions to be conducted. A feature of CRO is the increasingly stark asymmetry between the opponents. This is characterised, on the one hand, by a state with modern, powerful, well-equipped forces, but limited national interest or public support and severe political and moral constraints. On the other hand is a state or group of people with small, lightly equipped forces, unwilling to accept the norms of international law, possessing total commitment to their cause and showing scant regard for life and property. An interim definition of asymmetric warfare has been set out in MC 161: Those actions, which employ levels of forces and technologies to achieve a degree of effectiveness out of all proportion to forces employed, by seeking to exploit the vulnerabilities of NATO's civil and military infrastructures.

b. Joint Intelligence Preparation of the Battlespace. As in war fighting, intelligence in CRO will make use of Joint Intelligence Preparation of the Battlespace (JIPB). The JIPB factors considered in CRO include those used for planning for war fighting and others such as:

(1) The ethnic and demographic distribution in the [Area of Operations] AOO.

(2) The roots of the conflict and attitudes of the various groupings or political parties.

(3) The manner in which the cultural, economic, tribal or religious factors influence the conflict.

(4) Organised crime and other asymmetric threats.

3. *Commander's Handbook for an Effects-Based Approach to Joint Operations* states: Even if the joint force cannot locate the terrorist cell, terrorist actions could be prevented by interdicting the flow of money that finances the terrorists, weapons materials in transit, or the [Weapons of Mass Effect] WME assembly point. This understanding allows planners to devise courses of actions (COAs) that can be employed successfully against the terrorist system. In short, with a systems perspective, unified action—diplomatic, military, economic, or any combination of ways to attain greater unity of effort that has proved difficult in the past.

4. There are 145 Universal Joint Tasks associated intelligence and counterintelligence operations. Only the top level tasks are listed:

   a. SN 2 Develop National Strategic Intelligence, Surveillance, and Reconnaissance

   b. ST 2 Conduct Theater Strategic Intelligence, Surveillance, and Reconnaissance

   c. OP 2 Provide Operational Intelligence, Surveillance, and Reconnaissance

ENCLOSURE L

IRREGULAR WARFARE DEFINITIONS

> *Defense reform based on the field-earned knowledge of the Special Forces will begin with a doctrinal definition of irregular warfare, currently ill-defined by the Pentagon in terms of institutionalized strategy and terminology.*
>
>   — *"A Strategy for Irregular Warfare",*
>   Future Watch, December 2005,
>   Center for Strategic and International Studies

> *Going into this QDR [2006] and perhaps coming out, I would predict that we will have irregular warfare as well defined or as ill defined as we had homeland defense defined coming out of QDR [2001].*
>
>   - Major General Robert Durbin

1. USSOCOM and the Office of the Assistant Secretary of Defense for Special Operations and Low-Intensity Conflict hosted an IW workshop on 20 September 2005 for the purpose of reaching agreement on proposed DOD definitions for IW. There were several variants, which later lead to the approved Deputy Secretary of Defense definition stated in the IW roadmap.

> *"Irregular Warfare is a form of warfare that has as its objective the credibility and/or legitimacy of the relevant political authority with the goal of underming or supporting that authority. Irregular warfare favors indirect approaches, though it may employ the full range of military and other capabilities to seek asymmetric approaches, in order to erode an adversary's power influence, and will."*

This definition is the same working definition used by the USSOCOM and US Marine Corps for developing a multi-service operating concept for IW.

2. The study also found several other definitions and descriptions.

     a. Irregular *warfare* denotes a form of conflict where one or more protagonists adopts irregular methods. Irregular *troops* are any combatants not formally enlisted in the armed forces of a nation-state or other legally-constituted entity. Stability operations in this category include actions to counter irregular troops or forces employing irregular methods, counter terrorism, and assistance to friendly irregular forces. It is likely that in countering an irregular adversary the peace support activities mentioned will be conducted, but specific offensive and defensive operations will be utilised to counter that adversary and that the principles of COIN might be used. (NATO Allied Joint Publication 3.2, *Allied Land Operations*, 2d Study Draft)

b. **Joint Special Operations & Irregular Warfare** - The ability to conduct operations in hostile, denied, or politically sensitive environments to achieve military, diplomatic, informational, and/or economic objectives employing military capabilities for which there is no broad conventional force requirement. These operations may require low visibility, clandestine, or covert capabilities that are applicable across the range of military operations. They can be conducted independently of or in conjunction with operations of conventional forces or other government agencies, and may include operations through, with, or by indigenous or surrogate forces. *(Refined Joint Capability Areas Tier 1 and Supporting Tier 2 Lexicon*, 24 August 2005)

c. **Joint Irregular Operations/Warfare** – Joint Irregular Operations/Warfare involve conventional and special operations forces conducting operations to counter the activities of irregular forces. Joint Irregular Operations/ Warfare include elements of, but are not limited to, foreign internal defense and counterinsurgency, counterterrorism, unconventional warfare, information operations and stability operations undertaken to defeat adversaries who conduct activities and employ methods not sanctioned by international law or customs of war. Joint Irregular Operations/Warfare involve all elements of national power (diplomatic, informational, military, and economic) and as such are joint, combined, multinational, and interagency in its scope. Joint Irregular Operations/Warfare is generally protracted and requires sustained political-military willpower to effectively conduct. *(Refined Joint Capability Areas Tier 1 and Supporting Tier 2 Lexicon*, 24 August 2005)

d. **Joint Special Operations & Irregular Warfare** - The ability to conduct operations that apply or counter means other than direct, traditional forms of combat involving peer-to-peer fighting between the regular armed forces of two or more countries. The ability to conduct operations in hostile, denied, or politically sensitive environments to achieve military, diplomatic, informational, and/or economic objectives employing military capabilities for which there is no broad conventional force requirement. These operations may require low visibility, clandestine, or covert capabilities that are applicable across the range of military operations. They can be conducted independently of or in conjunction with operations of conventional forces or other government agencies, and may include operations through, with, or by indigenous or surrogate forces. (*Proposed Joint Capability Areas Tier 1 and Supporting Tier 2 Lexicon* (Mar 06 refinement effort results))

e. **Irregular Warfare** - The ability to conduct warfare that has as its objective the credibility and/or legitimacy of the relevant political authority with the goal of undermining or supporting that authority. Irregular warfare favors indirect approaches, though it may apply the full range of military and other capabilities to seek asymmetric approaches, in order to erode an adversary's power, influence and will. (*Proposed Joint Capability Areas Tier 1 and Supporting Tier 2 Lexicon* (Mar 06 refinement effort results))

f. Irregular warfare is warfare employing the tactics commonly used by irregular military organizations. This involves avoiding large-scale combats, and focusing on small, stealthy, hit and run engagements. (Wikipedia, July 2006)

ENCLOSURE M

GLOSSARY OF ABBREVIATIONS AND ACRONYMS

4GW	Fourth Generation Warfare
AOO	Area of Operations
AT	Antiterrorism
C4	Command and Control, Communications, And Computers
CA	Civil Affairs
Cbt	Combating Terrorism
CI	Counterintelligence
CIFA	Counterintelligence Field Activity
CIMIC	Civil Military Cooperation
CIST	Counter Ideological Support for Terrorism
CJCS	Chairman of the Joint Chiefs of Staff
CJCSI	Chairman of the Joint Chiefs of Staff Instruction
CM	Consequence Management
CMO	Civil-Military Operations
CNO	Computer Network Operations
COA	Course of Action
COIN	Counterinsurgency
COMSEC	Communications Security
CRO	Crisis Response Operations
CT	Counterterrorism
DEA	Drug Enforcement Administration
DHS	Defense Human Intelligence (HUMINT) Service
DIA	Defense Intelligence Agency
DISO	Defense Intelligence Support Office
DOD	Department Of Defense
DTIC	Defense Technical Information Center
EW	Electronic Warfare
FBI	Federal Bureau of Investigation
FID	Foreign Internal Defense
GPF	General Purpose Forces
GW	Guerrilla Warfare
GWOT	Global War on Terror
HN	Host Nation
HSE	HUMINT Support Element
HUMINT	Human Intelligence

GLOSSARY OF ABBREVIATIONS AND ACRONYMS

IA	Information Assurance
IDAD	Internal Defense and Development
INFOSEC	Information Security
IO	Information Operations
IW	Irregular Warfare
JCA	Joint Capability Area
JEL	Joint Electronic Library
JFC	Joint Force Commander
JIPB	Joint Intelligence Preparation of The Battlespace
JITF-CT	Joint Intelligence Task Force Combating Terrorism
JOC	Joint Operating Concept
JP	Joint Publications
JPME	Joint Professional Military Education
MASLO	Measurement and Signatures Intelligence Liaison Officer
MILDEC	Military Deception
MOOTW	Military Operations Other Than War
MSCLEA	Military Support to Civilian Law Enforcement Agencies
NATO	North Atlantic Treaty Organization
Ops	Operations
OPSEC	Operations Security
OSD	Office of the Secretary Of Defense
PA	Public Affairs
PD	Program Directive
PI	Public Information
PIR	Priority Intelligence Requirements
PSYOP	Psychological Operations
QDR	Quadrennial Defense Review
RAD	Revision Approval Draft
SAE	Special Areas of Emphasis
SO	Special Operations
SOF	Special Operations Forces
SSTR	Stability, Security, Transition, And Reconstruction
UAR	Unconventional Assisted Recovery
USCENTCOM	US Central Command
USG	US Government
USJFCOM	US Joint Forces Command
USSOCOM	US Special Operations Command

ENCLOSURE M

GLOSSARY OF ABBREVIATIONS AND ACRONYMS

UW   Unconventional Warfare

WMD   Weapons of Mass Destruction
WME   Weapons of Mass Effect
WOT   War on Terrorism

www.ingramcontent.com/pod-product-compliance
Lightning Source LLC
Chambersburg PA
CBHW080517290526
45790CB00006B/2209